D0422658

Liberal edu

LIBERAL EDUCATION

Critical Essays on
Professions, Pedagogy, and Structure

LIBERAL EDUCATION

Critical Essays
on
Professions, Pedagogy, and Structure

FREDERICK STIRTON WEAVER

Teachers College, Columbia University
New York and London

Published by Teachers College Press, 1234 Amsterdam Avenue
New York, NY 10027

Library of Congress Cataloging-in-Publication Data

Weaver, Frederick Stirton, 1939–
    Liberal education : critical essays on professions, pedagogy, and
structure / Frederick Stirton Weaver.
        p.   cm
    Includes bibliographical references (p.   ) and index.
    ISBN 0-8077-3063-7
    1. Education, Humanistic—United States.   2. Education, Higher—
United States—Curricula.   3. College teachers—United States.
4. Educational equalization—United States.   5. Educational change—
United States.   I. Title.
LC1023.W43   1991
378′.013′0973—dc20   90-21236

Printed on acid-free paper
Manufactured in the United States of America
98 97 96 95 94 93 92 91   8 7 6 5 4 3 2 1

Contents

Acknowledgments

I have been working with the ideas in this book for a long time, and in the course of working them out I have been fortunate to have received a lot of help from a range of friends, institutions, editors, and others. I will mention here only those whom I remember having made the most direct and tangible contributions to my putting these ideas together in these chapters, because otherwise the list is simply too long.

I very much appreciate the help of Alexander Astin, Peter Euben, Michael Ford, Penina Glazer, Frank Holmquist, Roberto Márquez, Adele Simmons, Miriam Slater, William Tierney, Stanley Warner, Serena Arpenè Weaver, and E. Frances White. Their contributions to these chapters may surprise and even dismay some of them. Special thanks go to Douglas Davidson, Michael Gross, and Rudolfo Torres, who worked closely with me in formulating some of the specific arguments in the book. Finally, I am deeply grateful for the skill, care, and patience of the Teachers College Press editors.

A part of the process of developing these ideas was to write them down for publication, and several journals published articles in which I presented earlier versions of my thinking. Although none of these chapters is actually a reprint of anything that I have published before, I gratefully acknowledge the permission to draw on those articles from the following sources:

"Academic Advising as Teaching," *Innovative Higher Education, 12* (Fall/Winter 1987), 22–25; by permission of Human Sciences Press (Chapter 5)

"Academic Disciplines and Undergraduate Liberal Arts Education," *Liberal Education, 67*, No. 2 (1981), 151–165; by permission of the Association of American Colleges (Chapter 1)

College Teaching, by permission of Heldref Publications

"Inquiry, Interdisciplinary Education, and Minor Programs of Study," *Issues in Integrative Studies*, No. 4 (1986), 37–56; by permission of the Association for Integrative Studies (Chapter 4)

"Introductory Statistics and General Education," *Journal of General Education*, 33, No. 4 (Winter 1982), 287–294; by permission of Pennsylvania State University Press (Chapter 8)

Journal of Black Studies, by permission of Sage Publications (Chapters 7 and 11)

"Scholarship and Teaching," *Educational Record*, 70, No. 1 (Winter 1989), 54–58; by permission of the American Council on Education (Chapter 9)

"Teacher Education, Liberal Education, and the Liberal Arts," *Action in Teacher Education*, 9, No. 1 (Spring 1987), 1–8; by permission of the Association of Teacher Educators (Chapter 6)

"Teaching, Writing, and Developing," *Journal of Higher Education*, 53 (September/October 1982), 587–592; by permission of Ohio State University Press (Chapter 9)

Finally, for the financial support that this effort has received, I thank the Exxon Education Foundation, the Gwyndaf Jones and Ariel Philips Fund, the Hewlett-Mellon Presidential Discretionary Fund, the Consortium for the Advancement of Private Higher Education, and the Council for the International Exchange of Scholars.

Introduction

General demographic and economic changes are the principal causes of the decline in the status of and support for higher education over the last two decades, especially in regard to undergraduate liberal arts programs. Nevertheless, there are conceptions and practices internal to the higher education enterprise at the undergraduate level that have contributed to the present malaise. These make it doubtful that a sudden, massive increase in private and public support for higher education, leading merely to the expansion of current structures and practices, would result in substantially better undergraduate education for students. This book is concerned with those educational changes that might make important differences. While more resources would certainly make the changes easier and less disruptive, the availability of increased resources is not the principal issue.

GOALS AND STRUCTURE OF
UNDERGRADUATE EDUCATION

The problems of undergraduate education are not simply stated. Vocationalism has been named as a culprit, but undergraduate education is, and should be, valuable for vocational purposes. In the United States, the bachelor's degree has always had a commercial and professional importance, as befits education in a nation with a materialistic culture and, as a consequence, considerable social mobility. Still, undergraduate liberal education should have some significant value beyond vocational training. What this value is or might be, however, has been so seriously obscured by colleges and universities themselves that current efforts to make a cogent case for liberal education on broader grounds—such as enhancing democratic citizenship, cultural heritage, civic responsibility, and the examined life—are too easily dismissed as desperate and self-serving attempts to find new sources of support.

1

Confusion and ambivalence about the goals in higher education are not new, but in recent times they have become more obvious and probably costly. Bowen (1980) discusses what such uncertainty about the sector's goals has for college and university budgets and develops what he calls the "revenue theory of costs." In his perceptive and somewhat humorous exposition, Bowen argues that, without clearly defined goals, the sector is unclear about what is being produced. As a consequence, costs in higher education are determined primarily by *revenues*. (This may be more amusing for economists than for others.)

One reason for the colleges' and universities' inability to articulate a coherent statement on the broader value of higher education is the lack of a tradition of critical scholarship on higher education. Liberal arts faculty, in their teaching and research, have had little interest in subjecting their own work and its settings to the same critical scrutiny that they apply to other social and cultural institutions. In addition to an understandable desire of faculty to avoid such exposure, liberal arts faculty do not respect education schools and faculty. Institutions of higher education, therefore, are not a high-status subject for research.

Without a strong legacy of systematic reflection on the organization of academic work and the institutions themselves, when administrators of liberal arts colleges and divisions have been confronted with the need to make a cogent case for undergraduate liberal education, they have had little to draw upon other than vapid catalogue copy and public relations experts from other sectors. In addition, cautious administrators have been reluctant to take certain directions in making the case. For instance, they have been constrained by the fear that heavy emphasis on critical and independent thinking as educational goals would have been seen (correctly) as incipient social criticism at a time when the market was most definitely not rewarding skepticism about broader aspects of the social order. As a result, those speaking on behalf of liberal education generally either argue that it really is vocationally useful or stay at a safe level of banality.

The radical student movement in the 1960s and early 1970s stimulated some healthful introspection but precious little in the way of thoughtful reform. How ephemeral was the effect of all that agitation and rhetoric is graphically illustrated by the fact that, within a decade, the meaning of the demand for "relevance" had turned into its opposite. Instead of colleges and universities defending themselves against accusations of fitting young people into, and thereby strengthening, extant systems of power and privilege, the same institutions quickly began to compete enthusiastically with each other to convince students how well they were able to do precisely that.

While the principal sources of recent challenges have been external to the academy, the expediency that has characterized institutions' rapidly changing declarations of purpose has highlighted their inability to identify what they are indeed about with any precision or credibility; to act upon it effectively, especially in regard to liberal education; and to demonstrate that they are accomplishing much of value in any dimension.

The volume of literature on higher education has grown enormously during the last decade and a half, but there appears in it very little enthusiasm for pursuing basic questions of conception and organization in a vigorously critical manner. General disquisitions on philosophy, purpose, and prospects all too often are blandly abstract or construct nostalgic myths about the 1950s and early 1960s, or earlier. These qualities in the literature, to a considerable degree, illustrate the writers' anxious reluctance to be controversial, especially pronounced among administrators and such institutions as the Carnegie Corporation, sponsor of the most prominent studies.

Another major type of higher education literature is being produced by a new academic breed of higher education specialist. The work done by these scholars has injected much needed rigor into the study of several important issues, generated useful data, and arrived at some provocative, nonintuitive conclusions. Yet the very methodological approaches that have led to these valuable contributions have at the same time limited the scope of these studies to fairly specific, "testable" hypotheses and managerial issues (Keller, 1985). Thus, while stimulating rethinking of several individual features of higher education, the critical engagement of more fundamental issues has, for the most part, been left to journalists and social critics within and outside of the academy. The work of these critics, however, has seldom addressed intellectual issues and in any case has not become a cumulative source of influence.

The purpose of this book is to clarify and promote what I see to be central purposes of undergraduate education, especially the elements of it regarded as liberal education. My basic argument, which pervades all of the chapters, is that the undergraduate educational enterprise must be defined primarily and most emphatically in intellectual terms. This does not render irrelevant other aspects of students' college experience, but it does mean that these other aspects are important primarily to the extent to which they support or obstruct intellectual development. In this advocacy, I advance a form of critical-inquiry education as especially promising, because it entails a pedagogy that directly and plausibly encourages the development of habits of mind to which all liberal education pays lip service but all too often discourages.

Of course, every purpose can be thought of as being simply instrumental in respect to some yet broader purpose, and enhancing democratic participation in society generally is the broader purpose that lurks under my intellectually defined goals of liberal education. Although most of the discussion in Part I of this book remains at the safer, more proximate level of educational goals (i.e., critical, independent thinking fostered by active involvement in one's learning), several of the chapters do speak directly to the direct and positive relationship between active democratic citizenship and the habits of mind nurtured by critical-inquiry approaches to undergraduate education.

In recognizing and valuing the connection between liberal education and democracy, I join a long tradition of U.S. scholarship. Even though some scholars regard heightened political involvement to be threatening (e.g., Crozier, Huntington, & Watanuki, 1975), this fear is not shared by most scholars of education, and especially of college and university education. There is a strong, consistent historical tradition contending that one of the central purposes of liberal education is to promote a tradition of democratic citizenship that emphasizes an ideal of responsible and active political participation, and this tradition cuts across a wide range of political identities (e.g., Bloom, 1987; Bowles & Gintis, 1976; Hook, 1946; Hutchins, 1936; Shor, 1980).

There is, of course, considerable disagreement among them about exactly what traits should be developed by college education in order to enhance democratic citizenship, and about how effectively higher education performs this function. But, whatever the writers emphasize—common culture, political self-awareness, an inquiring intellect, a knowledge of U.S. political institutions, experience in exercising choice—the promotion of the values and capacities for active democratic citizenship, and therefore a more democratic political order, has continued to be one of the most enduring and prominent criteria of excellence in undergraduate education. This consensus may not be very secure, however. In mainstream discussions of primary and secondary education, underselling the Japanese in international markets already appears to have overshadowed any democratic aspiration as a principal goal of education (e.g., U.S. National Commission, 1983; also see deYoung, 1989 for the historical relationship between economic goals and educational reform.)

The goals of intellectual development and democratic citizenship are both compatible and complementary, and efforts to improve undergraduate education in intellectual terms will directly enhance the democratic citizenship side of colleges' and universities' missions. While this aspect cannot be compromised, there are other vitally important conditions for successful democratic education, in addition to the curricular and intellectual considerations. The most important is the availability of higher education to all who can benefit from it, and the degree of that availability is an important measure of colleges' and universities' ability to support and enhance democratic citizenship. The issue of access is frequently couched in terms of higher education's function as a vehicle of social mobility. These terms implicitly accept a society that is characterized by substantial inequality. These same writers, however, also place a very positive value on some individuals' being able to move among the various layers of inequality, occasionally using Social Darwinist statements about meritocracy.

But this mobility cannot be universal if the structure of differential privilege behind the notion of social mobility is to be preserved. The social mobility that college and university education enables, therefore, can be constrained in two ways, by restricting access to higher education and by nurturing a hierarchical system of institutions that results in some college and university educations opening up far more opportunities than others. So efforts to increase truly democratic education entail removing obstacles to access while ensuring that the resulting access is to high-quality college and university education. (See Astin, 1982, for an excellent discussion of this issue.)

One last general observation about the chapters in this book concerns my approach to the various topics. Colleges and universities have developed to such a point and in such a manner that their internal processes are extremely important determinants of what is happening and what will happen in higher education. Some of these processes and structures (e.g., disciplinary organization of curricula, criteria for faculty appointment and advancement) are internal to the sector as a whole, and some are internal to individual university systems and institutions. External influences, of course, are still very powerful, especially in matters of overall financing, but the effects of external influences are mediated and shaped by established and even entrenched academic structures, practices, interests, and customs.

Although it is comforting to those of us who work in colleges and universities to attribute all problems and shortcomings to forces outside our control and responsibility, I consider this reading of causation to be woefully inadequate. As a result, I stress the internal organization of colleges and universities as a necessary beginning point for comprehending their responses to changing national and world conditions.

(See Clark, 1984, pp. 33–39, for a similar argument; also Weaver, 1980, who makes the same argument for a *very* different set of social processes.)

One problem with stressing internal relationships is that it can slide rather easily into voluntarism and calls for moral rearmament. While I do believe that in large measure the future of higher education is indeed in the hands of those directly involved with the sector, the organization of institutional power, faculty work, and student programs are not malleable and easily changed, either by individual faculty members and administrators or by an entire institution. Stepping out of well-defined grooves is risky in all callings, and academics and academic administrators are notoriously timid. Massive changes throughout the whole sector are not feasible (or possibly even educationally productive). For example, the change in the age composition of college and university undergraduates and the deterioration of employment prospects for Ph.D.'s in the liberal arts over the last few years have had very little effect on institutions' key academic organizations and practices. And even if these organizations and practices had been less resilient and the external changes had had strong effects, it would still be necessary to understand the way in which institutions' structures shaped and mediated those influences into eventual effects.

ORGANIZATION OF THE BOOK

Part I presents the intellectual and curricular issues of liberal education, with Chapter 1 establishing a background by outlining the historical development and current meaning of academic disciplines—the central intellectual and administrative units in virtually all liberal education in the United States. My use of history is not intended to construct an ideal out of the past, but rather to show the kinds of changes that have occurred and the ways in which the past needs to be transcended. The central argument is that academic disciplines as they exist today should be understood as primarily professional organizations, not categories of knowledge, and that this understanding is necessary to clear up confusion about the source of the consensus in the liberal arts about what is to be taught and how. I call the resulting system of power, preferences, and mores "disciplinary professionalism," a system that was in widespread operation by the 1950s.

No sooner had disciplinary professionalism become strongly established in colleges and universities than it began undergoing a series of challenges. Student revolts in the 1960s and the academic recession in the 1970s and 1980s challenged both the disciplinary patterns of academic life and the faculty authority that underlay those patterns. Chapter 2 describes the nature and results of these pressures on disciplinary curricula and faculty power.

With this background in mind, Chapter 3 suggests a definition of undergraduate liberal education that is not completely dependent on the disciplines but at the same time does not fall into the vacuousness that is characteristic of so much discussion about "interdisciplinary" education. This type of liberal education is generally known as "critical-inquiry education," and Chapter 4 discusses the curricular and pedagogical principles embodied in it.

The four chapters of Part I are thus general treatments of undergraduate liberal education and in this respect are different from the level of exposition in the six chapters of Part II. These discuss concrete and relatively straightforward applications of the conception of educational purpose and principles outlined in Part I.

Chapter 5 describes two curricular innovations that hold real promise for moving students' educational experience toward desired educational goals. There is good reason to believe that the innovations sketched here are financially and politically feasible in most colleges and universities. The major point, however, is not to push for these specific reforms, but rather to offer two examples that illustrate the modest level at which productive educational reform can be effected. Although visionary proposals are essential to maintaining high aspirations and a sense of proportion, arguments that any meaningful curricular change in higher education requires a full-scale revolution are misplaced and indicate a lack of imagination on the part of their authors.

The next three chapters of Part II address the implications of critical-inquiry education for three important facets of the curriculum. Chapter 6 is on teacher education, which is both intrinsically important and an excellent example of how intellectually vigorous conceptions of undergraduate education undermine hoary and arbitrary distinctions between liberal education and professional education. These distinctions, which benefit neither students nor the professions into which they will enter, are an obstacle to educational progress.

Chapter 7 deals with the place of a "new" subject matter—Black (or African-American) Studies—in the curriculum. When the curriculum is regarded in light of the principles of critical-inquiry education, the educational potential of such areas of study looks considerably stronger and more interesting than when seen through the lens of conventional curricula. Moreover, the conception of education em-

bodied in critical-inquiry approaches opens up important new strategies for successfully dealing with faculty politics.

Chapter 8 focuses on the introductory statistics course, notorious
among teachers and students for being the dullest, most deadening
course in the curriculum. I maintain that this situation demonstrates a
serious misunderstanding of the nature and importance of the course's
goals.

The last two chapters in Part II deal with faculty development, a
rather hapless term that describes a critically important facet of undergraduate education. Here again—this time from the point of view of
faculty members rather than of curricular goals—arises the argument
that teaching is primarily an intellectual act and active learning by
students requires active learning by faculty. As Chapter 9 contends,
too much of the debate about the proper role of scholarship for
teaching faculty continues to be informed by the implicit conviction
that undergraduate teaching is essentially the transmission of a fixed
body of information and techniques and that faculty scholarship
means disciplinary scholarship and no more. Both of these shibboleths
are serious obstacles to enhancing the status of undergraduate education, and it is important not to be trapped by them.

The last chapter in Part II is an empirical study of the content of
articles from social science college teaching journals and the reward
structure of different types of colleges and universities for faculty
writing and publishing about teaching. This chapter demonstrates that
this scholarly genre, the potential importance of which is discussed in
the previous chapter, is woefully underdeveloped and that faculty are
seldom encouraged to contribute to its development.

Part III consists of two chapters that deal with the noncurricular
aspects of democratic education mentioned earlier—access and quality. Although I do not treat the issue of access directly and generally,
Chapter 11 discusses the possibilities and problems historically black
public colleges and universities face in redefining their missions after
the end of legal segregation in higher education. These institutions
have been and continue to be vital parts of the higher education
system, offering educational opportunities to people who otherwise
would not have had them. In this sense, black colleges and universities
are preeminent democratic institutions, and their future has consequences that go beyond the individual campus, community, and state
educational system.

If access to higher education is to have educational and democratic significance, it must be access to quality education. The final
chapter of this book discusses the meaning and implications of varia-

ble quality among institutions of higher education, by emphasizing the strongly hierarchical organization of colleges and universities. The class-tracked nature of higher education is a property of the higher education system assiduously avoided in treatises and speeches ostensibly addressing quality in undergraduate education. I argue that the democratic side of any educational reform efforts is jeopardized if educational inequalities are not explicitly addressed. As opposed to curricular reform, the changes needed to improve this dimension of educational quality are not modest.

This book is part of a continuing, and occasionally raging, debate about higher education in the United States. As such, I welcome comments and criticisms that will help the debate be more productive.

PART I

Principles of Liberal Education

1

Liberal Education and the Rise of Disciplinary Professionalism

Liberal education has generally positive connotations among academics, but its meaning is extremely vague. The tacit definition is seldom more precise than "that which goes on in liberal arts colleges and divisions" (e.g., Hawkins, 1983; Zingg, 1983). Part of the vagueness stems from efforts to follow the student market, so that in the 1980s we heard a lot about "applied liberal arts." But the sources of the vagueness run deeper than that, certainly back to the classical curriculum of the early days of higher education in this country. At that time, near the close of the eighteenth century, liberal education was seen to have two distinct dimensions, and clarifying those two dimensions is important for interpreting current educational debates as well as for understanding the influences that have shaped current conceptions of what is educationally desirable.

CHANGING INSTITUTIONAL CONTEXTS

There is a persistent tendency by scholars of higher education to represent eighteenth- and early-nineteenth-century U.S. colleges through static models or "ideal types." This device, similar to social scientists' use of the term *feudalism*, has the unfortunate result of flattening the considerable variation and evolution among those early colleges. The colleges' small size and financial fragility meant that they necessarily reflected their local and regional communities and the religious denominations that sponsored them. In addition, there is the temptation to romanticize those colleges and ignore their authoritarian, dogmatic, and intellectually shallow nature. Aside from a few pockets of relatively high culture, the colonies and early republic were frontier societies in which the life of the mind, much less ideological diversity, was not highly valued, even when tolerated (Handlin & Handlin, 1970; Hofstadter, 1962).

In spite of these cautions, it appears that the classical curriculum of the early colleges quite consistently embodied two fundamental educational goals, the combination of which constituted the definition of liberal education. The goals were the development of mental faculties and the acquisition of liberal culture (Kolesnik, 1958; Rudolph, 1977). These two goals were graphically described in the famous Yale Report of 1828, where it was argued that the purposes of education concerned "the *discipline* and the *furniture* of the mind; expanding its powers, and storing it with knowledge" (quoted in Rudolph, 1962, p. 132).

In the domain of liberal culture (the furnishings), emphases on Greek and Latin texts and the Bible acquainted students with the body of knowledge seen as a necessary part of the definition of an educated, cultivated gentle*man* suitable for the ministry, learned professions, and leadership elite—all, of course, vocational goals. A modern exemplar of this liberal culture aspect is the list of people, places, events, and so on compiled by Hirsch (1987) and touted by him as that which educated people must know.

In the early colleges, however, this body of knowledge served a second purpose. Students translated these texts from one language to another, and by means of recitation and disputation were instructed in ancient languages, religion, mathematics, formal logic, and natural philosophy. These subjects had some liberal culture rationale, but they were also valued as a way to develop such mental faculties as attention, memory, and reasoning. The curriculum and pedagogical strategy were thus designed to achieve both the liberal culture and mental discipline goals of liberal education, which made sense in terms of then-current learning theory.

A combination of mutually reinforcing trends in the nineteenth century destroyed this neat confluence of theory and practice. Colleges began to employ a small core of permanent, career faculty—professors whose responsibilities were defined in terms of subject matter. Before this innovation, college faculties were made up of tutors who taught the entire curriculum to an entry-class cohort of students as they moved through the college. These tutors were usually recent graduates of the college who taught for only a few years before moving on to the ministry or other positions. By the third quarter of the nineteenth century, the outlines of current patterns of faculty employment were discernible, but they were not fully consolidated until the twentieth century (Finkelstein, 1984).

The incorporation of new subject matter into college curricula was closely related to the changing character of the teaching faculty. The natural sciences, modern languages, and modern literature had been included in the curricula of many colleges by the middle of the nineteenth century, and the social sciences were rapidly becoming differentiated and established as separate curricular entities by the end of the century. Linked to the expansion of the curriculum, pedagogical styles shifted toward seminar and lecture formats and forensic rather than deductive debates, and elective systems began to supplant unitary curricula.[1]

In light of current liberal arts self-images, there is definite irony in the fact that proponents of the earlier ideal of liberal education viewed these new subject matters, such as modern languages and literature, history, and the natural and social sciences, as intrusions that pandered to students' vocational interests. This illustrates the incompleteness of analyses that argue that the expansion of college and university curricula has been due to the explosive growth of knowledge. Certainly this accounts for some of the increases in subject matter taught in higher education institutions. On the other hand, many of the new subjects were not new knowledge but were simply knowledge that for the first time was considered appropriate to be taught in a college or university. More and more knowledge became institutionalized by the expansiveness of the university curriculum, and debates over whether a certain subject was or was not suitable for inclusion in the curriculum were often framed in terms of a subject's "practicality." The real debate, however, was about the social class of the student body deemed appropriate for higher education.

The rapid growth of public land grant institutions and private research universities at the end of the nineteenth century changed the context and forums of the debate over who should attend and what should be taught. The liberal arts colleges were eclipsed by the newer, more dynamic institutional forms. The old-style colleges that survived this sea change in higher education either transformed themselves into research universities or altered their curricula to serve as feeder schools for professional and graduate programs located elsewhere. Although liberal arts colleges with long histories have continued to be important for the education and socialization of privileged young people, in the twentieth century they have operated essentially as specialized branches of the research universities, adapting to educational changes from other sources rather than being a source of educational innovation in their own right.

The intention of the federal government in subsidizing public colleges and universities was unabashedly vocational. The Morrill Act of 1862, which granted federal lands to state colleges and universities, charged these land grant institutions to teach applied branches of learning, especially those related to agriculture and the mechanical arts. On the other hand, the new private research universities of that day (e.g., Johns Hopkins University [1876], Clark University [1887], University of Chicago [1890]), inspired by a highly selective (and often inaccurate) understanding of German universities and institutes (Perkins, 1984), were devoted in large part to the expansion of knowledge and the training of graduate research specialists. Their dedication to these purposes was so great that several of these new universities wished to eschew undergraduate education altogether, but they found that this was not financially feasible.

In spite of their initial differences in purpose and auspices, however, the influences of competition, growth, and emulation led to considerable convergence between land grant universities and private research universities, and quickly the differences between them became more a matter of extent rather than of kind. The leading land grant universities (e.g., Michigan, Wisconsin, Illinois, California) established doctoral programs in the natural and social sciences and eventually in other fields, and the private research universities started up or expanded professional programs, even in such fields as education and business. By the 1920s and 1930s, the major differences between the two types of institutions resided principally in the wider range of undergraduate programs in the land grant institutions, reflecting their public sponsorship and the fact that their student bodies were more representative of the population as a whole.

Veysey (1965) argues that the fundamental outlines of the current U.S. system of higher education were clearly visible by 1910, and although I would argue that the date was actually one or two decades later, there is no question that much of what continues to be characteristic of U.S. higher education was readily apparent in the early twentieth century.

Some of these features looked very unusual to Continental and British academics. For example, student undergraduate study programs in the United States were much less specialized than in Europe, where the responsibilities for imparting educational breadth were vested in elite secondary schools that screened student admissions and graduation by social, financial, and academic criteria, permitting only a very few to be eligible to enter higher education. On the other hand, while the study programs of U.S. colleges and universities were less specialized, the number of baccalaureate degree programs (and even of baccalaureate degrees) offered by U.S. institutions was extremely large, and probably ludicrous, by European standards. European models of higher education, as in many other fields, exerted such hegemony among Eurocentric academics in the United States that many continue to be apologetic about U.S. colleges and universities; see White and Ahrens (1989) for a good antidote to the belief that European university systems are generally superior to those in the United States.

In addition to their relatively democratic and populist character and willingness to teach a great variety of subjects, U.S. colleges and universities increasingly organized their curricula into discrete modular courses, with course credit hours and the elaborate bookkeeping procedures necessary to keep track of students' academic progress. Within these individual courses, combining the functions of teacher and examiner appeared suspect to European academics, because it seemed to pit the students directly against the professor as well as to work against maintaining the impersonal, disinterested application of high academic standards.

The system of U.S. higher education, therefore, was open, flexible, sensitive to the market, and consistent with the highly individualistic ethos of the nation (Rosenblatt, 1989). A direct consequence of its decentralized, competitive character in a society with definite differences in wealth, power, and status was that it also was a system made up of institutions of quite uneven quality. This fact has been frequently ignored. Clark (1987), for instance, discusses how competition creates an institutional hierarchy but remains silent on the social class implications. By the early years of the twentieth century, it was already clear to contemporary observers that some colleges and universities were superior to others. An institution's location in this hierarchy reflected the status of those whom the institution served (see Chapter 12 for an analysis of some implications of this hierarchy). While there has been some institutional mobility in this prestige ranking of colleges and universities, both upward and downward, during the last 70 or 80 years, the hierarchy has flourished.

In 1973 the Carnegie Council on Policy Studies in Higher Education first organized the institutions of higher education into major categories. Related Carnegie agencies have subsequently issued two updated editions, and the most recent information, from 1987, is given in Appendix A (Carnegie Foundation, 1987a). Although the order in which institutions are presented in the Carnegie classification scheme is not crudely from "best" to "worst," there is no question that the classification contains strong judgments about quality.

In another key element in the development of U.S. higher education, the organizational convergence of the private research universities and the public land grant institutions in the early twentieth century contributed importantly to the growth of academic disciplines. These institutions promoted, sponsored, and directly subsidized national disciplinary societies and journals (Geiger, 1986). The means by which knowledge and faculty professional reputations were organized was considerably less centralized than the corresponding process in Europe. In the United States, each discipline established a national organization that was open to membership by virtually all interested, even though they were eventually dominated by academics. Even though neither African-Americans nor women were especially welcome, this was a much more open situation than European national (and frequently government-sponsored) academies, which were defined more broadly by subject matter but to which only a very few scholars were invited to belong.

National disciplinary journals, however, constituted a more centralized mode than sponsorship by individual departments and institutes, as was common in Europe. Nevertheless, some key disciplinary journals in the United States continue to be sponsored by individual departments. For example, in economics, Harvard's *Quarterly Journal of Economics* and the University of Chicago's *Journal of Political Economy* are both disciplinary journals open to contributions from authors in other institutions.

Academic disciplines became the central categories of knowledge, administrative units, and curricular identities, designating the content and defining the meaning of undergraduate as well as graduate programs in the liberal arts. Academic disciplines were also the primary means for organizing the professional lives of faculty members and quickly became vehicles of faculty professionalization.

ACADEMIC DISCIPLINES AS PROFESSIONS

Although we all know, at least in some general sense, that academic disciplines are a set of conventional categories of knowledge, it is less well appreciated that these categories also embody and rely upon a system of power relationships. Disciplinary conventions are defined and enforced by departments, learned societies, scholarly journals, degree structures, and grant agencies. That is, academic disciplines, like all aspects of social life, are multifaceted phenomena, with one vitally important facet being their functioning as professional organizations.

In a manner analogous to other professions such as medicine and law, disciplinary professionals organize and create specialized knowledge and transmit it to others. In the name of creating and transmitting knowledge, disciplinary professionals control the training and certification of disciplinary competence, reserve a range of jobs for certified practitioners, work to maintain standards by dispensing sanctions and rewards, and insulate themselves from the judgments of outsiders in all of these activities. The Ph.D. awarded by university departments is the reigning professional certificate, and through control mechanisms like journals, learned societies, and degree structures, disciplines sustain internal hierarchies and define a particular set of intellectual and other activities as professionally legitimate.

The intellectual and institutional foundations of disciplinary professionalism can be traced back centuries, but the transformation of higher education along the lines of academic disciplines was spurred by a broader and more recent movement outside the academy: the rise of the urban middle class and its ambitions and career expectations. That movement rapidly consolidated into what Bledstein (1976) has so aptly called the "culture of professionalism."

The traditional professions of medicine and law, after the post–Civil War disintegration of elitist local guilds, were reorganized into state and national professional groups based on what the participants saw as meritocratic principles. The ministry continued to decline as a college-educated profession and as an influence in colleges. Meanwhile, a whole range of middle-class occupational groups actively and self-consciously sought to become professions. Morticians, dentists, pharmacists, librarians, veterinarians, school teachers, engineers, architects, social workers, and public administrators are examples of occupational groups whose members made concerted efforts to control their occupations in the name of eliminating quackery and establishing authority for sound, professional practice.

The historical reasons for the widespread professionalization efforts at this time have begun to be explored in suggestive ways (Bledstein, 1976; Glazer & Slater, 1987; Haskell, 1977; Larson, 1977), but in this surge of scholarly interest, the significance of the relationships between the professional projects of academics and those of other occupational groups has not been sufficiently recognized.

Before proceeding with this discussion, it is important to note that I define a profession by the special set of institutionalized occupational controls that regulate the means of entry, standards of practice, and competition within and among occupations. This definition is used primarily in economics, which has uncharacteristically been the academic discipline most critical of professional pretensions. Economists generally analyze professionalization as a mechanism to restrict and control the operation of the freely competitive market for the advantage of the particular occupational group (e.g., Kessel, 1958).

This somewhat cynical view of professionalization clarifies what functionalist approaches in sociology have obscured, but it needs to be refined a bit. The necessary refinement to the definition of a profession requires no more than to add bachelor's or advanced degrees from colleges and universities as entry requirements, thus distinguishing professions from other occupations (e.g., trades) that also are formally controlled by other means. This distinction avoids the definitional inadequacies criticized by Veysey (1979).

The successful professional projects were those that fastened onto the emerging university as the means to train and certify a standardized competence, and the most successful projects were able to enforce graduate degrees as necessary vehicles for entry into the profession. Delegating professional training to colleges and universities entailed struggling simultaneously against amateurism, apprenticeship systems, and proprietary schools. These struggles were more successful in some cases than in others, depending only in part on the character of the occupations and much more on the political influence that could be brought to bear on behalf of the occupational groups. The rewards for driving out amateurs and rival training systems were substantial for those in a position to reap them.

All of this, however, is only one side of the professionalization projects. Vesting training and certification in universities, monitored by professional associations, was possible and effective if and only if the resulting symbols of competence were honored by employers, clients, patients, and other customers for the professional services. There is little point in controlling the supply of a quality service if the demand for that service is not assured. This was a problem, because even though aspiring professional groups magnified and exploited people's fears and insecurities about health, social order, sex, race, and culture, they could not rely on the unprofessional public to respect the professional certificate to the proper extent.

If the public at large could not be adequately convinced, state legislatures were capable of being persuaded to enforce the needed recognition by closing off whole sets of activities to all but the certified (see tables in Council of State Governments, 1952). In some cases, governmental licensing of occupations was the prior condition for raising standards, that is, for requiring practitioners to have college and university degrees. In addition to suspending the freely competitive market, all levels of government contributed significantly to a considerable number of professional projects by creating demand for appropriately certified professionals, either directly by employing them or indirectly by creating procedures and requirements that forced others to employ them.

The drive for professionalization was a major impetus for the creation and expansion of the modern university and for the transformation of undergraduate colleges in the late nineteenth and early twentieth centuries. Not only did the expansion of higher education require more teachers, but the new importance attached to these institutions by ambitious professions and professionals meant that the functions of training and culling students required *qualified* educators. Thus academics, in their professionalization efforts, were able to manipulate to their own advantage the same symbols of competence, merit, and specialization used by others.

Nevertheless, while the academics' language was similar and their general interest in professionalizing instruction was apparently congruent with those of other professions, the manner in which leaders of the newly founded national disciplinary associations conceived of their professional projects was not so harmonious with the aspirations of students and nonacademic professional groups. Academics managed to define competence, merit, and specialization in terms appropriate for professionalizing *research* rather than teaching, thus significantly contributing to the institutionalization of knowledge production primarily in universities. No doubt some of this was due to the influence of the German academic model as well as to an effort to distance college and university teachers from primary and secondary school teachers. Nevertheless, the consequence was that teaching generally, and undergraduate teaching in particular, remained low-status professional work.

It is no surprise, then, that the organization of disciplinary graduate programs, designed to train research professionals, was strongly influencing undergraduate curricula by the end of the nineteenth century. The elective system of student course selection, which supplanted the prescribed curriculum, was another step in the development of disciplines and faculty professionalization. Although the principal significance of the elective system might at first glance seem to be freeing student choice in course selection and areas of studies, these choices were necessarily from a menu set by the faculty. The most important effect of this curricular innovation, therefore, was to free *faculty* from the prescribed curriculum and to allow them the choice of what to teach. (This is analogous to the observation by Marx in 1843 that freedom of religion in the United States freed the *state* rather than the citizenry from religion.)

During the early decades of the twentieth century, the increasing distinction between lower-division and upper-division undergraduate curricula allowed a compromise between proponents of broad, liberal culture studies and those advocating specialized work in disciplinary and professional curricula. The first two years were reserved for what was becoming known as "general education," while disciplinary majors and minors and professional study dominated the upper-division years. This bifurcation of the undergraduate program, encouraged by the development of junior colleges, was a key step in the penetration of the undergraduate curriculum by disciplinary professionalism, although the corresponding changes in administrative arrangements were not worked out until the 1930s (Rudolph, 1977).

The entry of the visual and performing arts, as the newest and least professionalized of the liberal arts disciplines, is still being contested in some places. Although arts faculty are often put into a separate professional school, when they are included in the liberal arts, they are constantly subject to criticism about standards from colleagues in more established disciplines. Ackerman (1973) and Morrison (1973) provide adequate, but uncritical, discussions of the place of visual and performing arts in higher education.

It is especially important to understand that, in the process of faculty professionalization, *each academic discipline* came to constitute a distinct professional body. While adequate for some purposes, the usual "academic profession" category is too general to identify some of the most interesting features of the process.[2] Although disciplines were housed side by side in educational institutions and played similar roles in the preliminary training of disciplinary and nondisciplinary professionals, the disciplinary particularism of highly professionalized faculty members was already firmly established in the largest and most prestigious research universities by the 1920s.

Their curricula and organizational structure were already segmented into autonomous departments, divisions, schools, and colleges. This device enabled the universities to maintain simultaneously a set of internally inconsistent goals—liberal culture and utility, specialization and breadth, research and undergraduate teaching—that could nevertheless coexist within the same institution as long as their pursuit was effectively separated.

By the late 1940s and early 1950s, disciplinary departments, formally equal in the institutions' organizational charts, had become the point of intersection between disciplines and institutions, and the avenue of professional advance and recognition was outward from the department to national disciplinary associations, journals, and colleagues—far from undergraduate students, class schedules, college committees, academic deans, and other irritating institutional demands that promised fewer professional payoffs. The proper role of the institution in this scheme of things (and one that the "best" institutions accepted and pursued in order to enhance their reputations and external funding) was to support, honor, and compete for individuals to whom disciplinary bodies had accorded professional recognition.[3]

The faculty identification with the discipline over the institution, of course, was not universal. Now, as it was then, such identification is strongest in the research universities, and as one moves down the hierarchical rankings of institutions by prestige and looks at colleges and universities that have fewer educational resources per student and serve working- and lower-class students, the institution and client orientation increases relative to disciplinary and peer orientation. In spite of this, surveys repeatedly find that disciplines rather than types of institution are the major determinant of variations among faculty attitudes and opinions (Bowen & Schuster, 1986).

PROFESSIONAL AUTONOMY IN THE ACADEMY

The dependence of faculty professionalization on colleges and universities rather than on national or state governments required substantial autonomy by disciplinary departments within the institutions. The achievement of the necessary autonomy called for more influence than was available to the fragmented disciplines. Metzger (1965) gives the best description of how this was accomplished, and he shows that, in the first decades of the twentieth century, several national disciplinary associations vainly tried to establish the primacy of purely professional criteria in faculty personnel decisions, but their impotence was unequivocally demonstrated in some notorious cases of faculty firings.

Cooperation was clearly necessary to dilute the power of college and university administrations and governing boards. In 1913, representatives of the American Economic Association, the American Political Science Association, and the American Sociological Association took a preliminary step with the founding of the American Association of University Professors (AAUP), encompassing all disciplines. The AAUP's central purpose was clearly expressed in the classic 1915 report of its Committee on Academic Freedom and Tenure:

> The responsibility of the university teacher is primarily to the public itself, and to the judgment of his own profession; and while, with respect to

certain conditions of his vocation, he accepts a responsibility to the authorities of the institution in which he serves, in the essentials of his professional activities his duty is to the wider public to which the institution itself is morally amenable, [quoted in Metzger, 1965, p. 409].

General civil libertarian convictions did have some role in the formation of the AAUP, but the central point was academic professionalization, that is, reserving certain crucial realms (curriculum, research, and personnel) to the judgment of professionally certified competents, who were seen to be the disciplinary faculty. (Cadwallader [1983] gives an excellent analysis of academic freedom and tenure that links them to substantive issues of teaching and research.) These professional disciplinary faculty, and *not* administrators, trustees, or legislators, were seen to be the only qualified interpreters of the interests of the "wider public."

The struggle by academics for professional autonomy within colleges and universities was similar in substance to the licensing efforts of other occupational groups, but, in sharp contrast to the predominant situation in other professions, the principal employers of academic professionals are academic professionals themselves. As soon as the AAUP's principles of academic freedom and tenure became general practice, it was professional historians, biologists, economists, philosophers, and so forth who trained and subsequently hired most new professionals in their fields. Therefore, each disciplinary profession directly controlled the principal demand for and the supply of certified professionals.

As a consequence, there are no bases for continuing conflicts between professional associations and professional schools, nor are overt political interventions (e.g., licensing) required to insure the market for the certificate. This almost pure form of professional colleague orientation (as opposed to client orientation) obscures the professional character of academic disciplines, even to academic disciplinarians. It also raises another type of question. In a frequently reprinted article, Kessell (1958) argues that the geographic dispersion of medical practitioners made the cultural homogeneity of physicians important for coordinating and maintaining their professional monopoly in the national market. Therefore, there were tangible pecuniary reasons for making it more difficult for anyone who was not a white Protestant male from at least an upper-middle-class background to enter the profession.

There is no question that the professionalization of academia, with its stress on merit, did open the professoriate to people who had formerly been excluded, in particular Jews, Catholics, and women. Nevertheless, it is disturbing that the peculiarly strong market control exercised by disciplinary professionals in the academy did not cause them to be considerably bolder in opening their professions to others.

TRIUMPH OF THE PROFESSIONAL PROJECT

As already noted, disciplinary professionalism, along with its research ethos, was already firmly established in leading research universities by the end of the First World War, and it became diffused throughout U.S. higher education in the next three or four decades. It was in the 20 years after World War II, however, that academic disciplines became the principal, even exclusive, way to organize legitimate curricula and faculty professional work. This is the period in which higher education enjoyed public confidence, rapid increases in enrollments, large-scale research projects funded by public and private sources, and shortages of qualified faculty.

Shulman (1979), relying mostly on Ladd and Lipset's (1978) survey data, argues that the rise in faculty salaries and general status during this period attracted to the professoriate young people from higher social strata than had previously been the case at least beyond a handful of elite institutions that had always exhibited strong class bias in recruiting faculty members. (See Blau, 1973, on this last point.) Thus, while a college education was vaunted as a vehicle of upward mobility, college teaching became less so. Moreover, it is also likely that increasing numbers of faculty from more privileged backgrounds contributed to the occupation's professionalization.

These were the institutional conditions that enabled the place of academic disciplines to be developed, crystallized, and confirmed in the postwar decades (Baldridge, Curtis, Ecker, & Riley, 1978). Attributing this development and confirmation wholly to external influences short-circuits the crucial mediating linkage—the unparalleled rise of faculty power within institutions and the increasing authority of these institutions to arrange their internal affairs with only indirect and distant intervention by outside constituencies. The broad and favorable changes in the sector's fortunes, insulating them from the need to respond to students' curricular preferences, rapidly led to greater faculty autonomy, especially in matters of curriculum, personnel, and research. But this internal shift in power expressed itself as the rise of the academic disciplines only because disciplinary professionalism was already sufficiently established as a tendency and direction. There is no inherent reason for favorable external conditions to have had this result.

Once again, however, it is important to note that this triumph was uneven within the stratified system of higher education institutions. In schools at lower levels of prestige and prosperity, administrators, trustees, and government bodies still had considerable influence over key academic decisions. If institutional governance is regarded as the combination of two distinct administrative types—collegial and managerial (Austin & Gamson, 1983)—the balance of power in lower-status institutions continued to be tilted much more toward the managerial. For instance, bureaucratic control in the community colleges more resembles the governance patterns found in secondary and primary schools than in research universities or elite liberal arts colleges.

In the last 30 years, however, the entire pattern of disciplinary professionalism, in terms of both faculty control and curricular organization, has been profoundly challenged throughout higher education, and we will explore some of the consequences of these challenges in the next chapter.

2

Challenges to Disciplinary
Professionalism

As described in Chapter 1, the crystallization of disciplinary professionalism occurred in the 1950s and early 1960s, when favorable external conditions gave faculty in colleges and universities the opportunity
to develop what were for them the most desirable definitions of work
organization and standards. The institutionalization of disciplinary
professionalism was not uniform, of course, but it dominated the
definition of academic work and was solidly based in the leading
institutions: undergraduate colleges serving the children of the privileged, and the top research universities closely linked to the federal
government and major corporations through research contracts and
graduate training programs. Kerr (1972) gives the quintessential expression of purpose and rationale for top public research universities.

STUDENT REVOLTS AND
INSTITUTIONAL COMPETITION

In predictable dialectical fashion, these institutional developments
produced their own negations. Although the general oversubscription
of higher education insulated institutions from student market pressures in curricular matters, strong student reactions to the type of
education they were receiving became frequent in the late 1960s and
early 1970s. The protests most often occurred in the "best" colleges
and universities, where disciplinary professionalism was strongly established and students' backgrounds made them less awed by their
school.

There is considerable irony in the results of the student reaction.
The most important consequence in undergraduate education was to
dismantle general education and breadth requirements. The demise of
the lower-division requirements freed faculty from the need to teach
outside their specialized areas or even to talk with colleagues from

other specializations, reduced the importance of the local campus to an ambitious faculty member, and left disciplinary majors virtually unchallenged as the only coherent and systematic curricular entities.

As noted in Chapter 1, the changes made in the name of freeing students from requirements actually were more important in freeing professors from the requirement to offer certain courses. Many student radicals, in pushing for the relaxation of lower-division requirements, must have been puzzled by the ease with which they found enthusiastic allies among highly professionalized faculty with little or no interest in undergraduate education. Moreover, the power and attraction of academic professionalization subsequently proved strong enough to bring many of these New Left student activists comfortably into the professional fold as academics (Jacoby, 1987).

A second type of response to disciplinary professionalism and changes in undergraduate teaching practices was the establishment of alternative institutions and programs that attempted to provide the styles of education for which many students were calling. Most of these institutions and programs, whose organizations and curricula were nondisciplinary or even antidisciplinary, were attractive primarily to the confident children of middle- and upper-class parents, in spite of institutional rhetoric to the contrary. In any case, many of them lasted only a short time, and even the most durable have exercised little influence on the direction of undergraduate education. Whereas these new programs and institutions professed the hope of serving as laboratories of experimentation or as change agents, their actual role has been little more than to increase the range of market choice in higher education, especially for those who already had the widest range of choices. Altogether, alternative programs and institutions have remained rather polite alternatives to what has continued to be the educational mainstream.

These two challenges to the established order in higher education during the 1960s and early 1970s—student revolts and alternative programs and institutions—did not result in significant changes in the disciplinary organization of undergraduate education or touch internal patterns of authority.

ACADEMIC RECESSION

Beginning in the 1970s, all of the positive factors that had enabled the development of faculty control over curriculum, personnel, and research—namely, increasing enrollments, widespread respect and confidence, private and public financial support for institutions and research projects, and a shortage of faculty—quickly became their opposites. At that time it looked as though there would be a serious academic depression in the 1980s and 1990s, severely undermining disciplinary professionalism.

One aspect of the academic recession that was potentially dangerous to the political position of faculty was the sudden and dramatic increase in the importance of institutional budgetary policy. Decisions about curriculum, personnel, and research, although vital for disciplinary professionalism, do not make up the whole terrain of institutional power. Faculty control over general institutional budgetary matters has never been very strong, and with the need to reduce or at least contain institutional costs (including faculty salaries), one might have expected an eclipse of faculty authority on campus.

Salaries, Inflation, and Authority

Whether the academic recession manifested itself primarily through a decline in student enrollments, research grants, legislative subsidies, or private giving, the way it was registered within an institution was as a financial shortfall. This result is the famous bottom line, and faculty salaries themselves constituted about 40% of colleges' and universities' bottom-line expenditures. The financial pressures on institutions dictated a significant reduction (or at least containment) of costs, including faculty salaries. The salary issue was a likely source of a direct confrontation between faculty and administrators, and one that faculty in most institutions were not in a favorable position to win.

The reason general financial pressure did not lead to a more serious assault on faculty authority in colleges and universities across the nation was because it was not necessary. The fortuitous presence of high rates of inflation created a mechanism by which the reduction or containment of institutional costs in general and faculty salaries in particular was eased. At the same time that colleges and universities were beginning to run into financial difficulties in the 1970s, the nation was experiencing high and sustained rates of inflation along with stagnating or falling levels of production. The whole phenomenon came to be known as "stagflation." In part triggered by the energy crisis, inflation was a global phenomenon throughout most of the 1970s. In colleges and universities, inflation disrupted established patterns on both the revenue and expenditure sides of institutional ledgers and relentlessly pushed up operating costs at precisely the time that the specific forces of the academic recession were putting sharp downward pressures on institutional revenues. This grim picture of financial squeeze was standard fare in speeches and articles at the time, but the conventional portrayal distorts the effect of inflation by ignoring the opportunity it provided for adjusting institutional costs to accommodate income difficulties.

The idea that inflation substantially benefited colleges and universities might seem odd, if not downright bizarre, to those who were directly involved in trying to meet rapidly rising costs with insufficient revenues. But by stepping back from the bitter struggles that became so characteristic of higher education budget management and taking a comprehensive and even somewhat cynical look at budgetary data, inflation can be seen to have been a means for achieving substantial budgetary relief.[1]

The most obvious source of such cost savings is the extent to which inflation reduced the real burden of colleges' and universities' long-term debt. A good part of this debt was incurred during the 1960s and early 1970s to finance new buildings and physical facilities, and as the debt and its scheduled repayments were fixed in money terms, inflation reduced the real value (purchasing power) of these monetary magnitudes and thus in effect subsidized college and university debtors at the expense of their public and private creditors.

While the size of these effects was substantial, I will focus on other, less well recognized mechanisms by which inflation led to relief in the operating budget. Inflation is the general rise of prices, but because prices do not change by the same amount, inflation permitted changes in relative prices that would have been very unlikely under conditions of price stability. In analyzing the way in which inflation allowed for the pattern of relative price changes yielding budgetary relief, I will concentrate on faculty salaries. They were a large part of total costs, and their determination held explosive potential for conflict and change in campus governance, yet they eventually became the source of most of the savings derived from the opportunity offered by inflation.

As a first step in the analysis, it is vital to recognize that inflation, in and of itself, does not necessarily result in lower real earnings for faculty, or indeed for anyone else. For instance, during the inflation and general economic slump of the last half of the 1950s, average faculty salaries rose more than three times faster than the consumer price index (CPI) and over two and a half times faster than the salaries of engineers (U.S. Bureau of the Census, 1975). But that was a period of buoyancy for colleges and universities: Rising enrollments, public faith, government research grants, and shortages of qualified personnel enabled faculty to make real income gains despite inflation and recession.

In addition to there being no general imperative for inflation to inflict losses on faculty, the labor intensiveness of higher education and the difficulty of demonstrating productivity growth (or even of defining the product) could lead one, with plausible assumptions, to expect that costs in higher education, led by wages and salaries, must inevitably rise faster than costs in other sectors. Baumol (1967) gives a concise and lucid presentation of this model, the logic of which clearly influenced the analyses of Carnegie Commission (1973) and Breneman (1981), among others.

In the 1970s, however, when all the positive conditions for faculty influence within colleges and universities had begun to turn negative, the market position of faculty, along with that of other higher education professionals, deteriorated markedly. Poor market conditions for faculty, therefore, reflected the general decline in the position of colleges and universities as an economic sector, a decline that forced institutions to reduce costs as well as they were able.

In addition to its intense use of professional labor, higher education's vague goals, pursued with an uncertain technology, also make it a peculiar and distinctive industry. For this reason, costs in higher education tend to be more influenced by available revenues than they are by any internal logic of production or notion of efficiency.[2] While colleges and universities thus may have more latitude than profit-seeking firms regarding where and in what proportions to reduce costs, at a more general level they are like any other enterprise in that they can lower costs only by reducing quantities purchased and/or prices paid for purchases.

In dealing with outside contractors (e.g., the telephone company or suppliers of paper, power, books, and typewriters), there is very little scope for reducing prices, so quantity reductions (e.g., energy conservation measures, fewer library acquisitions, less paint) are the typical cost saving responses.

In the case of faculty, however, traditions of job security and formal tenure as well as the need to maintain a reputation for financial soundness and for quality (of which the student-faculty ratio is a prime indicator), mean that faculty layoffs are used with extreme reluctance and only as a last resort. In inflationary times, then, it was easier and safer to reduce the price component of total faculty salary budgets.

This does not mean, of course, that reducing faculty salaries is either easy or safe. In economic theory's special world of freely competitive markets with perfectly mobile factors of production, one would expect the reduction in demand for faculty, *ceteris paribus*, to lead to a reduction in faculty salaries. This had the greatest direct effect in the case of the salaries of new hires, where the lag in training for the professoriate is so lengthy that the supply of new faculty entering the profession was determined more by the availability of even part-time positions than by faculty salaries. This situation of job competition, rather than wage competition, is an excellent example of the argument made in Thurow (1975), which emphasizes job openings rather than wage levels as the principal determinant of labor allocation and employment. Engineering, computer, and business faculty, however, were exceptions to this phenomenon; their ready access to employment outside the academy meant that institutions could not take advantage of inflation in setting these individuals' salaries.

On the other hand, salaries for continuing faculty are determined by negotiation, explicit or tacit, within each institution and system, rather than by the operation of impersonal market forces. Without clear and cogent evidence of extreme financial exigency, current money salaries are accepted by all parties as the bare minimum for next year's salaries. Although market weakness can affect the eventual bargain struck, during the 1970s recession it had not, in most institutions, diminished the faculty's political power to the extent that money salaries below current levels were feasible. If prices had been stable between 1973 and 1980, real faculty salaries (i.e., the purchasing power represented by faculty earnings) could only have been reduced by lowering faculty money salaries, and the direct confrontation with faculty power would have required an unequivocal breaking of faculty authority that would have had repercussions in all aspects of faculty work, including disciplinary professionalism.

Inflation, however, allowed institutions to avoid the potentially disastrous consequences of such confrontations by dramatically changing the context in which faculty salaries were set. Although current money salaries might no longer have been an acceptable minimum in time of inflation, money salaries that rose but did not keep up with the rise in the prices of consumer goods (and thereby represented a reduction in purchasing power, or real income) were legitimate, albeit not desirable possibilities.

Table 2.1 shows that these possibilities were indeed what consistently occurred between 1973 and 1980. Faculty salaries, which constituted 42% of college and university operating budgets in 1973, grew by 46.5% between 1973 and 1980, but they lagged far behind the 81.4% increase in average prices, as measured by the Consumer Price Index (CPI). This lag was of such magnitude that by 1980, purchasing power

TABLE 2.1 Structure and Growth of College and University Operating Budgets

Budgetary Category	Percentage of Total Budget, 1973	Changes in Prices, 1973-1980 % Incr.	% of CPI
Personnel compensation	**82.0**	**159.2**	**87.8**
Professional salaries	58.0	146.0	80.5
Faculty	*42.2*	*146.5*	*80.8*
Administrators	*8.5*	*144.1*	*79.4*
Librarians	*2.0*	*145.5*	*80.2*
*Others*ᵃ	*5.3*	*145.3*	*80.1*
Nonprofessional salaries	15.0	168.5	92.9
Clerical	*5.4*	*166.8*	*92.0*
*Others*ᵇ	*9.6*	*169.5*	*93.4*
Fringe benefits	9.0	207.1	114.2
Contracted services and supplies	**18.0**	**198.3**	**109.3**
Servicesᶜ	7.3	153.0	84.3
Supplies and materials	3.5	205.8	113.5
Equipment	2.5	175.4	96.7
Books and periodicals	1.7	205.6	113.3
Utilities	3.0	317.1	174.8

Consumer Price Index (CPI):181.4%

ᵃIncludes graduate assistants (2.7%) and extension and public service workers (2.6%).

ᵇIncludes technicians (1.5%), craftspeople (1.0%), students (2.0%), service workers (4.0%), and operators and laborers (1.1%).

ᶜIncludes data processing and equipment rental (1.4%), communications (1.5%), transportation (0.7%), printing and duplication (0.5%), and miscellaneous (3.2%).

Sources: D. Kent Halstead, *Higher Education Prices and Price Indexes* (Washington, DC: Government Printing Office, 1975), p. 141; and D. Kent Halstead, "Higher Education Prices and Price Indexes: 1980 Update," *Business Officer* (October 1980), n.p.

of faculty salaries was only a bit more than 80% of what it was in 1973. This consequence was no doubt influenced by the common practice of considering next year's cost-of-living salary increase as essentially a residual, the remainder left after subtracting from estimated revenue the total for outlays on needed purchases of goods and services and current salary figures. But no matter what procedure was used, inflation allowed the continuation of familiar, even traditional, rhythms of salary increase—promotion and merit for individual faculty members, acknowledgment of general faculty aging, and granting salary adjustments for cost of living—while real faculty salaries declined sharply.

This does not necessarily imply deliberate manipulation, and faculty by and large went along with it. Their acquiescence was not because they did not understand what was happening. The extent to which faculty salaries did not keep up with the rise in the prices of

consumer goods was meticulously reported in higher education journals (e.g., Hansen, 1980; Fact File, 1981a, 1981b), and the resulting
decline in real salaries—just short of 20% between 1973 and 1980—was
very large and constituted a substantial retrenchment for the sector as
a whole. Nevertheless, even faculty belonging to unions perceived the
rather abstract and diffuse erosion of their real income and the impersonal, "equitable" mechanism that distributed the burdens to be an
acceptable compromise in a threatening situation in which, with young
people seeking to enter academia and only slight mobility of experienced faculty out of it, they had little bargaining power. Hansen
(1986) provides a good review of these years of salary history, despite
his odd periodization. Inflation, therefore, offered a soft option in
hard times.

The faculty were not the only employees in higher education who
experienced declining real salaries in the 1970s. The figures in the last
column of Table 2.1 show that all college and university personnel
experienced sizable losses of real income between 1973 and 1980,
although nonprofessionals fared somewhat better than professionals.
Like faculty salaries, the real salaries of nonfaculty professionals, with
skills specialized to higher education, declined nearly 20% in those
years, although this had a smaller budgetary impact.

As serious as these real-income losses were for individuals, it is
imperative to recognize that, for institutions, these represented declining real *costs* (prices paid for labor services). The first column of Table
2.1 shows their proportional importance in the operating budgets of
colleges and universities in 1973, and even a casual perusal is enough to
demonstrate the financial significance of the decline in real costs to
employing institutions.

Finally, Table 2.1 also presents the major categories of college and
university costs in which prices rose more rapidly than the CPI. The
relative importance of these especially inflation-prone items was so
small, however, that their rapidly rising prices did not offset the gains
from the decline in the real salaries of faculty and other professionals.

In order to illustrate the magnitude of the net budgetary savings
derived from the uneven changes in prices, I calculated some hypothetical budgetary figures in order to estimate the total budgetary
savings reaped by privately controlled four-year colleges, due to inflation. These calculations are explained and discussed in Appendix B,
and they are presented there in Table B.1. The result of these calculations was that the cost savings due to the relative price changes allowed by inflation was around $809.5 million, over 8% of 1980 operat-

ing budgets, and these savings would have paid the salaries of tens of thousands of faculty members at the average faculty salaries prevailing in independent four-year colleges during fiscal year 1980 (Hansen, 1980).

The form in which colleges and universities realized these cost savings was as money that did not have to be spent while still purchasing the 1973 volumes of goods and services (including labor services). The proclivity of colleges and universities to spend all available revenues meant that these cost savings were used, and institutions increased expenditures in other budget lines, especially on such activities as admissions, fundraising, and student services, without serious reductions in direct educational resources (although real educational expenditures per student did decline). An additional use of these savings was to lower the real price of education to students and parents by raising tuitions and room and board charges less than the increases in the CPI and by aggressively discounting "list" tuitions beyond federal subsidies. Both policies thus made private higher education more attractive than it would have been if its costs to students and parents had risen equally with other prices.

These are the major elements of inflation's contribution to smoothing colleges' and universities' transition during the 1970s from the prosperity, growth, and optimism of the postwar years to the much leaner, even bleak prospects of the 1980s and 1990s.

With the relatively stable prices and guarded optimism of the late 1980s, colleges and universities have been trying to catch up in both faculty salaries and tuitions. Even so, this does not mean the effect of the inflation during the 1970s was merely ephemeral. College and university debt outstanding in the early 1970s is not going to recover its previous real value, and even if real salaries in the sector do return to or even surpass previous levels, this does not offset the financial benefit derived by the institutions during the 1970s. There is no question that the inflation of the 1970s enabled institutions to reduce real costs and reallocate resources internally in order to make the change to a situation much less congenial for those who work in higher education.

Because inflation enabled colleges and universities to reduce faculty salaries without having to break, in an explicit and devastating manner, the faculty's political power within academia, the conditions for disciplinary professionalism were not seriously damaged by the immediately financial consequences of the academic recession. But there were other aspects of the recession that more directly threatened the faculty's control over the disciplinary organization of teaching.

Student Market Power and Institutional Dependence

With the reversal of the conditions that had fostered and extended disciplinary professionalism, there were good reasons to expect that not only would disciplinary professionalism be weakened by an assault on faculty control over curriculum, personnel, and research, but that the disciplinary organization of those aspects of faculty work would be severely weakened.

The logic of this position is straightforward. As the size, financial health, and even survival of institutions became increasingly dependent on recruiting and retaining students from smaller cohorts and differing backgrounds, the relationships between faculty and administrators would shift toward unambiguously accepting the principle that the faculty's primary responsibility is to design and implement instructional programs attractive to students. In the words of the final report of the Carnegie Council on Policy Studies in Higher Education (1980),

> Students will be recruited more actively, admitted more readily, retained more assiduously, counseled more attentively, graded more considerately, financed more adequately, taught more conscientiously. . . . The curriculum will be more tailored to their tastes. . . . This may well become their Golden Age. [p. 53]

The students exercising this market power, moreover, would be undergraduate students, and demographic changes suggested that middle-class students between the ages of 18 and 22 years would constitute increasingly smaller proportions of the smaller enrollments (Hodginson, 1983). The "new" kinds of students—including older, part-time students and those from less privileged economic and more diverse ethnic backgrounds—together with many of the more traditional student constituencies pushed by the economic uncertainty of the late 1970s and early 1980s, would choose more applied, vocational curricula over liberal arts programs.

The slack market for new liberal arts faculty would reduce the size and number of liberal arts graduate programs. In conjunction with the sharp reduction in private and public research funds, this would render a severe blow to disciplinary professionalism's core, which is made up of the research graduate departments that train new liberal arts faculty.

Professional education at both the undergraduate and graduate levels, on the other hand, would continue to do a brisk business, and faculty in those fields, who have consistently been less interested in disciplinary professionalism or in extending faculty authority, would be considerably strengthened in numbers and internal political influence. Other new elements in institutional politics were the large numbers of part-time faculty and faculty specializing in teaching remedial skills, none of whom had a compelling stake in strengthening disciplinary professionalism.

Faculty unionization likewise would not be of much help in retaining the hegemony of academic disciplines, because, like faculty senates and the AAUP, unions are most effective when they are perceived by their members to be neutral in respect to intra-institutional struggles among disciplinary (and other interest) groups. Moreover, the need to deal with unions, repeated budgetary crises, governmental regulations, student consumerism, and so on contributes to the supplanting of administrators with faculty backgrounds by labor relations specialists, lawyers, fundraisers, financial experts, information processors and manipulators, student counselors, and others with highly specialized skills important for the new market conditions for higher education (Baldridge et al., 1978). The faculty, as a consequence, would have less direct influence on them than on their more academically oriented predecessors, and this new breed of higher education manager would be considerably less sympathetic to or impressed by disciplinary professionalism.

These are the pressures, tendencies, and conditions, then, that would allow and even require institutions to reassert control over faculty work, at the expense of disciplinary professionalism. By the depression scenario, institutions would have to cater to students rather than to faculty and, if faculty were to try to retain their professional work patterns, trustees, state legislators, and, above all, college and university administrators would assume control and set the directions in this new context.

Instead of shifts in the curriculum toward professional and vocational subjects coming at a time of general expansion (e.g., the early years of the land grant colleges), colleges and universities would have to reallocate contracting resources to meet the interests of a changing type of student. This would lay bare the conflicts of interests between students and liberal arts faculty professionalism precisely at the time that the faculty position was very weak, institutions' need for students was very strong, and the availability of public and private sources of financial resources was, at best, undependable.

Predictions similar to this were made by a number of observers (e.g., Carnegie Council, 1980; Carnegie Foundation, 1977; Riesman, 1980; Stadtman, 1980; Weaver, 1984). To some extent, these predictions have proven to be accurate, but the forces have not led to qualitative changes in the undergraduate curriculum, and disciplinary professionalism has been very resilient. These adverse conditions have affected colleges and universities less than expected. The actual patterns require some elaboration.

The first notable element in the explanation is that the academic depression and the decline in the numbers of undergraduate students in the 1980s have not been nearly as serious as gloom-and-doom forecasts in the 1970s indicated (Baldridge, Demerer, & Green, 1982; O'Keefe, 1985, 1989). The downturn has been a recession and not a depression. This milder form of hardship had less impact on an entrenched disciplinary professionalism, which had established a strong hold on the consciousness of even the general public. This is well illustrated by the way in which the anxiety felt by college students in the very uncertain times of stagflation and sharply declining middle-class employment opportunities led those students who did enroll in liberal arts programs to favor familiar areas of study and to avoid nontraditional programs that might put them at a competitive disadvantage after their baccalaureate years (Krukowski, 1985). This strengthened the "core" disciplinary curriculum relative to experimental or interdisciplinary curricula (with women's studies programs being perhaps the most significant exception).

Reflecting the aforementioned widespread loss of public faith in colleges and universities, a number of important constituencies, including state legislators, federal officials, and parents, began to exert considerable pressure on the sector to demonstrate that it was doing a good job at what it was doing. Articulating "what it was doing" was in itself very difficult, and it has resulted in confusion, waffling, and self-serving rhetoric. This is true for education in general, as attested to by Rossides (1984). Nevertheless, the demands for accountability that focused on basic academic skills (e.g., reading, writing, computing, and so on) did not immediately threaten disciplinary professionalism.

Aside from basic skills, however, colleges and universities had developed very few terms beyond the disciplinary ones for talking about quality, and these terms were therefore vigorously employed for external constituencies as well as for internal discussion. The quality of an institution's departments of economics, biology, literature, business, history, and so on was used as a major element in its definition of overall quality. These are measures of inputs rather than outputs, of course, but, irrespective of the meaningfulness of the measures or indeed of how particular institutions fared in the use of any particular measure, the major point is that those who are demanding account-ability by and large accept the terms of disciplinary professionalism.

Moreover, the power of disciplinary curricula in academia is fur-ther illustrated among those colleges and universities that are not elite private colleges or successful research universities (i.e., the institutions attended by most undergraduates). In many of these institutions, disci-plinary departments and curricula are being more than reaffirmed, they are being actively created and enhanced. These are the institu-tions where the pressures from limited resources, the fear of declining enrollments, and the need to respond to outside constituencies by demonstrating and raising perceived quality are the greatest. As a consequence, these institutions are using the established principles of disciplinary programs in undergraduate curricula as a way to enhance their status and academic credibility.

Administrators do this for personal career purposes, of course, but trustees assent to (and occasionally initiate) this effort because of very real concerns about institutional competitiveness in the shrinking market for students and funds. The forms of disciplinary professional-ism, therefore, have become so firmly established as a standard in higher education that fears of a real academic depression channeled institutions into the conventional, or prudent course. The success of disciplinary professionalism is demonstrated by its ability to identify itself as that prudent path.

Efforts at institutional emulation were aided by the worsening liberal arts academic labor market in two ways. New Ph.D.'s from graduate departments in leading research universities frequently had to accept jobs in institutions much farther down the academic pecking order than they had selected two decades earlier, thereby bringing the mores of academic professionalism to places that had been less influ-enced by it. And the narrowing of promotion and tenure opportunities has allowed many institutions to raise or even initiate promotion and tenure standards in disciplinary research. They have gone in this direc-tion in part because of the desire to emulate, but also in part because, in the effort to raise standards of faculty retention and promotion, re-search seems to be much more easily assessed than is teaching quality, which remains rather elusive in respect to an accepted definition, to say nothing of the reliable scales necessary for measurement and comparison.

This brings us to one of the most interesting points. The general acceptance of disciplinary professionalism as an indication of institu-tional and educational quality among such external constituencies as administrators, trustees, legislators, and potential students has been the acceptance of a form that does not require significant faculty control over the curriculum and work conditions. Even though the historical development of disciplinary professionalism was both a product and a vehicle of increasing faculty authority, the recent wave of disciplinary professionalism is penetrating institutions and fields new to its influence at the same time that a greater degree of bureaucratic management of colleges and institutions, as predicted by scholars of the academic recession, restricts faculty control.

These changes, which are often accompanied by unionization and other procedural bureaucratic mechanisms, have not occurred in all institutions; they have been concentrated in those colleges and universities located in the middle and toward the bottom of prestige rankings, where client- or student-driven exigencies have retarded the development of the peer or collegial modes of governance typical of disciplinary professionalism (Clark, 1987; Ruscio, 1987). For example, in their management styles, governance, and general campus intellectual life, community colleges look increasingly like secondary schools rather than public research universities.

Faculty control has been bent in some places and hedged in at many others; in some upwardly mobile institutions, both public and private, the anomalous nature of the change is graphically illustrated by administrative "leadership" pushing reluctant faculty into disciplinary professionalism, a mode of academic operation that 50 years ago required and supported faculty autonomy. The success of disciplinary professionalism as an ideology of academic quality means that it now has a life of its own and no longer requires the degree of faculty institutional authority that it necessitated during the years of its struggle to define faculty work. The willingness of other agents within higher education to advance the forms of disciplinary professionalism means that its manifestations, including the disciplinary curriculum, can survive and even be established without the faculty having sure and consistent control over curriculum, personnel, and research decisions.

This point is illustrated by the selective manner in which upwardly mobile institutions (public and private) choose what features of the more prestigious institutions to emulate. While the trappings of disciplinary professionalism, along with publication imperatives, are encouraged and proudly displayed, these aspiring institutions are often reluctant to engage more actively in the recruitment of women and minority faculty and students, to expand participatory governance, to regard dissent as educationally productive, and in general to enhance (or at least tolerate) a more diverse, pluralistic institutional environment. These characteristics of a vital, confident, high-quality institution are less attractive to the aspiring.

A somewhat anomalous consequence of the uneven nature of emulation is that, within the widespread effort to increase faculty research and scholarship, elite institutions' tolerance for heterodox scholarship makes them considerably more comfortable and feasible for radical scholars than institutions whose students better represent the interests being advocated by dissenting scholars. As a consequence, elite colleges and universities have been the target of shrill political attacks (e.g., Kimball, 1990) posing as curricular criticism. Whatever the outcome of this criticism, for now, at least, it remains true and somewhat ironic that upwardly mobile institutions, though they promote scholarship and limited forms of disciplinary professionalism, can be dangerous places for highly professional, publishing dissidents.

Heightened disciplinary professionalism in upwardly mobile institutions may impart a new type of intellectual vitality to them, as is noted in Chapter 3, and the penetration of an authentic research ethos, as part of the emulation, may undermine the standardization necessary for effective bureaucratic control of faculty work. But even with the possibilities of such a dialectic, emulation still probably stifles curricular innovation.

Over a decade ago, the Carnegie Foundation (1977) forecast that basic curricular innovations would begin to be exported from the periphery to the core, reversing the historical direction of flow. Apart from some new educational delivery systems, that expectation now seems to have been erroneous. On the other hand, the innovative energy in liberal education evident in the core, or commanding heights of elite institutions, has not been impressive either. This is exemplified in Conrad and Wyer's (1980) review and discussion of criticisms of Harvard University's new, unimaginative general education program.

CONCLUDING REMARKS

In this chapter, which included some of the technical aspects of inflation and budgets, I have shown how, in spite of real battering, the organization and practices of disciplinary professionalism have managed to survive, in fairly good shape, the challenges of student revolts, experimental colleges, and academic recession. But working in higher education in the late 1980s and early 1990s is very different from what it was at higher education's high point of, say, 1970. The effect of unfavorable external influences, and especially the academic recession, has been to increase the curricular similarities among institutions while at the same time heightening the differences among institutions in regard to the general tone and other intangibles of faculty work. While teaching loads, sabbatical and leave opportunities, and other formal aspects of faculty work appear to have changed only slightly if at all, faculty work in other less concrete aspects has deteriorated markedly, especially in nonelite institutions. Even allowing for special pleading and the self-pity to which faculty are prone, there is no question that some very important aspects of faculty work conditions—including collegiality, autonomy in teaching and research, and scheduling flexibility—have deteriorated rather drastically over the last 20 years.

This dynamic, referred to as the "deadening constraints of austerity and diminished expectation" (Bowen & Schuster, 1986, p. 115), is of particular concern for those who worry about the ability of academia to attract high-quality new faculty when, beginning at the end of the 1990s, large numbers of new faculty recruits will be needed. Bowen and Schuster (1986) and Clark (1987) have contributed important analyses of this set of problems, noting as well that the financial incentives for entering the professoriate are modest, especially since the dramatic decline in faculty salaries during the 1970s. The principal attractions of academic work are different, however, and the decline in the quality of work conditions for most professors may discourage the entry of able people more than the decline in earnings. (Also see Austin & Gamson, 1983; Meléndez & de Guzmán, 1983; and Yuker, 1984.)

The rise in the numbers of women attending graduate school and teaching in colleges and universities, and the sag in the absolute numbers of men in both areas are suggestive. By the 1980s, around 34% of the professoriate were women; however, they accounted for only 27% of the full-time faculty, and their proportional representation among tenured faculty and faculty at prestigious colleges and universities was even lower (Bowen & Schuster, 1986). One must ask whether women's high rates of entry into liberal arts graduate programs and into college and university teaching, while men turn away from it, indicates a profession *already* declining in status, influence, and remuneration?

This question about women in academic careers leads naturally to others. If women are entering in increasing numbers, why is African-American and Latino representation in graduate programs and the professoriate declining? Is this a class phenomenon, in which a middle-class background is necessary for seriously considering the professoriate as a career, while those moving up from lower down in the social order head for more directly remunerative occupations?

Returning now to the principal theme of this chapter, the academic recession of the 1980s and 1990s is in itself unlikely to encourage significant academic reform. This is consistent with the reading of the 1930s by Henry (1975), who argues from the evidence that, during the Great Depression, "cutbacks were taken without basic alterations in structure and where traditional practices were disrupted, they were given priority in restoration" (p. 33).

While the political conditions of its expansion and welfare have changed, disciplinary professionalism is alive and well, and the next two chapters extend the discussion into the disciplines' intellectual and pedagogical properties.

3

Categories, Contents, and Knowledge: Toward a Reconsideration of Liberal Education

In analyzing the role of disciplines in undergraduate curricula, the professional model of disciplines offers a much more satisfactory explanation for their evolving and overlapping intellectual contents than do efforts to define disciplines by intellectual essence. The attempts to list distinctive intellectual characteristics of disciplines (e.g., subject matter, methods, and so on) are directly analogous to the 1940s and 1950s scholarship of the sociology of the professions. In this enterprise, much effort went into defining professions by listing sets of traits specific to certain occupational activities, traits that "explained" (i.e., justified) professional status and income. Johnson (1972) cogently criticizes this scholarly tradition and the comfortable functionalism that underlies it, but it is interesting to note that this approach to understanding professions is older than functionalism and should be considered to be a forerunner.[1]

ACADEMIC DISCIPLINES AND KNOWLEDGE

While the search for objective traits justifying professional privileges has been severely challenged by more critical approaches in the sociology of the professions, it appears to be alive and well in scholarship on academic disciplines, in spite of the trouble people have in applying it with precision or cogency (e.g., Becher, 1987; Broido, 1979; Fethe, 1973). A frequent way to avoid confronting this problem is to assume that academic disciplines are categories based on intellectually substantive distinctions (e.g., Clark, 1987).

44

Like the sociologists' traits of professions, such an approach to the study of disciplines begins by implicitly accepting at face value disciplinary professionals' assessments of their own activities and worth. Moreover, such an approach consistently fails to represent accurately how disparate are the specialized activities that are lumped together under one general rubric (such as history, philosophy, sociology, and biology) or to discriminate adequately among, for example, astronomy and physics, mathematics and philosophy, historical sociology and social history, anthropology and sociology, and even economics and business administration. In a similar vein, are ecology, urban studies, biochemistry, American studies, and geography *real* disciplines? These problems are considerably less formidable when one considers academic disciplines to be primarily professions, a large part of whose activities center on controlling the supply of and creating demand for qualified practitioners.

The conception of academic disciplines as professions does not deny their distinctive intellectual characters; various disciplines obviously do address different types of knowledge in different ways (Becher, 1984). Nor does my argument about disciplines deny the progressive moment for colleges and universities represented and furthered by the establishment of disciplinary professions in the late nineteenth and early twentieth centuries. There is no question that it significantly enhanced the intellectual character of undergraduate education.

As an integral part of the more strongly intellectual nature of the educational enterprise, the research ethos of disciplinary professionalism contributed significantly to the dominance of collegial governance in colleges and universities, where it developed real strength. Research and scholarship are much less susceptible to standardization and bureaucratic management than is teaching, and the emphasis on scholarship promoted the looser, less hierarchical types of governance that characterize high-status institutions.

The intellectually more serious nature of colleges and universities can easily be exaggerated, however, for the presence of other goals overriding the intellectual ones were clearly demonstrated by admissions policies that emphasized "character" in order to limit severely or exclude completely academically able but "undesirable" students like Jews, African-Americans, and women. Geiger (1986) provides a good discussion and list of sources on restrictive admissions practices, although, as in most such discussions (e.g., Levine, 1986), he hardly mentions the experience of African-Americans. Perhaps those authors believe that African-Americans were so far outside the mainstream of

U.S. life that their exclusion can simply be taken for granted, not needing explicit mention, much less analysis. In any case, we can see a replay of these protective ploys in elite colleges' and universities' current retreat from strictly academic admissions criteria, in order to limit the admission of Asian students.

Even with this serious caveat, however, the growth of intellectual seriousness was clear. At the same time, when one emphasizes the professional function of academic disciplines, it is also clear that questions about each discipline's intellectual coherence are important within the disciplines only to the extent that they serve the interests of research professionals. These interests require a definition of what a particular category of disciplinary professional does, and the more sharply this line can be drawn around a specialized expertise, the more convincing a case can be made for those research professionals within the boundary. But even in the upper reaches of disciplinary professionalism, standards of precision are not very high. Boundaries remain amorphous and subject to rapid and opportunistic redefinition when a growing field of inquiry, with promise of substantial employment and grant opportunities, looks as though it might fall outside the discipline. Occasionally these developments, whose genesis is often from outside the academy, lead to the birth of a new discipline.

Definitions of disciplinary content are vague, intellectually arbitrary, and change over time, but they do exist. The disciplinary departments of major universities, through their members' prominence in graduate training, national disciplinary organizations, editorial boards of journals, and advisory positions in funding agencies, are the principal arbiters of disputes about which side of the boundary particular questions, issues, methods, and views are located on. These departments exert a profound influence on what is or is not legitimate at a particular time, an influence that permeates higher education and professional work defined by discipline in all settings. The curricula of the leading graduate departments are the best indications of what new areas of intellectual activity are being approved for disciplinary sponsorship.

So, what are the implications for meaningful liberal education? The conversion of the liberal arts into a group of specialized disciplines for conducting research has qualitatively changed the meaning of liberal education. This is not acknowledged frequently enough, but, even when it is, seldom is it understood that the division of knowledge into supposedly discrete categories appeared possible and productive only because of the common stance toward knowledge that underlay and informed the research-oriented disciplines. This conception of knowledge, for the lack of a better term, I will call "positivism," although perhaps it is more properly called "realism," following Churchill (1983). It was clearly articulated as early as Bacon and Descartes, but truly flowered in the late nineteenth century with the triumph and prestige of positive science. It is here, in the positivist approach to knowledge and in the consequent understanding of the teaching function, that we can find a vitally important source of liberal education's changed meanings.

The positivist argues that, while the acquisition of knowledge requires sound methods (e.g., doubt as a path to certainty), knowledge itself is, in a very concrete sense, external to the knower, and the knowing subject and the content of knowledge are independent and only incidentally social in character. By this view, therefore, the purpose of education is to acquaint students with the facts and with the intellectual tools needed for the discovery of additional facts.

The idea from the positive sciences of objective, empirically based knowledge permeated the social sciences and history in the twentieth century and significantly influenced work in literature, philosophy, and wherever scholars aspired to the paradigm of experimental science. The optimism of this paradigm, integral to nineteenth-century liberalism, is very appealing: Human progress is seen to depend primarily on the advance of tangible knowledge. Knowledge grows incrementally but cumulatively and surely, as systematic research uncovers and records new facts and maps new intellectual terrain. In doing so, new knowledge is discovered for transmission to students.

As I have already noted, the development of research-oriented disciplines and the conception of positive knowledge were crucial in developing in colleges and universities a definition of purpose couched in what we now understand to be intellectual terms (Geiger, 1986). We can argue about the extent to which these terms have been realized in practice, but modern colleges and universities appear intellectually very serious when compared to their early nineteenth-century counterparts. As noted in Chapter 1, the old-style colleges were dominated by religious dogmatism and authoritarian modes of pedagogy and governance, and the faculty were often recent graduates who, while waiting for a ministerial position to open up, desperately tried to maintain some semblance of order inside and outside the classroom (Handlin & Handlin, 1970). It is equally important, however, to recognize that, because of these changes, liberal education became something that had only the barest connection with older meanings.

GENERAL EDUCATION AND COVERAGE

Although tainted by self-serving myth and by nostalgia for lost intellectual unities and social exclusiveness, an attenuated form of the
liberal education spirit survives in the notion of general education.
Areas of study such as literature, history, classics, religion, the rem-
nants of philosophy not incorporated in natural and social science
disciplines, and other unclaimed parts of the classical curriculum did
eventually undergo professionalization and become disciplines. In the
1920s, scholars in this disparate group of academic fields, which came
to be collected together under the umbrella label of "humanities"
(Veysey, 1978, 1979), became a self-conscious force in academic politics known as the General Education Movement.

Reacting to the high status of positive science and to the rewards
of specialization, aided by World War I patriotic fervor to teach
students the U.S. democratic heritage, and often supported by administrators trying to contain departmental power in the institution, the
movement succeeded in legitimizing required general education core
courses in a large number of institutions. These core courses, including
a few Great Books programs, were chiefly for lower-division students
and were but a pallid resurrection of the liberal culture component of
liberal education. In many other institutions, however, general education advocates had to settle for a distribution requirement, usually
involving students' taking a variety of introductory disciplinary
courses and perhaps a foreign language. The entry of visual and
performing arts into large numbers of curricula during the 1920s and
1930s further complicated the identification of what an educated person should know.

While this emphasis on the liberal culture side of general education
still required that students engage in some types of "mental discipline"
(e.g., attention and memory), the broader sense of mental discipline
that had been contained in the older conception of liberal education all
but atrophied. This was reflected in and advanced by the positivist
attack on the nineteenth-century psychology of mental faculties. The
work of Edward Lee Thorndike and his colleagues in the early twentieth century not only dismantled the hollow tenets of the psychology
of mental faculties, but was interpreted as proof that there were no
general intellectual skills. The conclusion, therefore, was that there
were only specific information (facts) and techniques to be known
(Cremin, 1961; Hofstadter, 1962).

As noted in Chapter 2, by the 1960s, a more sophisticated understanding of the social role of knowledge severely undermined the

consensus necessary to sustain ambitious general education efforts, and students' resistance to superficial survey courses in, say, "Western Civilization," allied with the faculty's increasingly rigorous disciplinary professionalism and skepticism about the intellectual merits of what was being taught, destroyed not only core courses but also the distribution requirement compromises in most colleges and universities. This left the disciplinary major as the only relatively systematic part of students' academic programs (or at least systematic in respect to faculty design). The recent resurgence of general education efforts is due to low enrollments in humanities courses, the reassertion of administrative authority, and the pressing need to enhance higher education's legitimacy in the eyes of various publics. This is not unlike the strengthening of the classical curriculum in the face of the challenge of Jacksonian populism 150 years ago.

Even though both core courses and distribution requirements are returning to undergraduate curricula (Gaff, 1983, 1989), it is revealing to see how educationally stunted are the public debates surrounding them. These new general education efforts continue to be requirements defined in terms that stress the liberal culture ("necessary body of knowledge") side of liberal education, which is compatible with positivism. That is, students are to acquire a certain set of information and techniques from an established corpus of material, an enterprise that could be expressed in terms such as *coverage* and *breadth* and that emphasizes the external, objectified character of knowledge.

Although directed at secondary education, Hirsch (1987) and Ravitch and Finn (1987) provide excellent statements of this conception of liberal culture and general education. Cheney (1989) avoids the simplistic Trivial Pursuit character of these two works, but her approach is clearly informed by a complementary understanding of the purposes of education. The Great Books of the Western Tradition, as proposed by Bennett (1984), Bloom (1987), and others, is a variant of the same essential knowledge theme; and, while it has more educational promise than the first, its proponents' presentations still concentrate on lists rather than the more difficult and important task of delineating the questions that might inform undergraduates' explorations of the books and the contexts in which they ought to be set for general education.

Bloom's (1987) book is a lament about U.S. culture and politics, and his analyses and prescriptions for higher education are extremely vague and suffused by nostalgia for an earlier and putatively superior kind of higher education. The nostalgia in Jacoby's (1987) work is very similar, albeit from a different political perspective; and Wolff (1987) gives an outstanding review of Bloom's (1987) book. Bennett's (1984) terseness and generality obscure the intellectual goals presumably contained in his proposed bibliography of great works. One is left with the uncomfortable feeling that all these authors subscribe to the argument identified with the faculty of St. John's College: These books bring their own contexts, and any effort to place them in some interpretive framework is unnecessary, suspect, and presumptuous.

These essentialist convictions are not restricted to one side of the narrow spectrum of U.S. politics. The argument about general education during the Reagan Administration, between Secretary of Education William Bennett and the Stanford University faculty, was conducted entirely in terms of what the list of people, places, dates, events, and titles should include, not about how they should be approached. DeParle and Mundy (1989) provide another example of an extremely limited conception of general education held by some who are critical of what they see to be a politically conservative agenda espoused by advocates of the great books and icons of Western civilization. On the other hand, it is odd that the advocacy of Great Books programs is so closely identified with political conservatism, for despite their Eurocentrism and misogyny, many of the ideas in that canon are (or could be) the bases of profoundly radical critiques of Western culture and society (Euben, 1990; Kates, 1989).

The intellectual and educational questions about distribution requirements, whether they are merely introductory courses for disciplinary majors or offered expressly for the general education program, are often subordinated to interdepartmental competition. Nevertheless, the educational value of courses designated to satisfy a distribution requirement, even including introductory disciplinary courses, cannot be dismissed out of hand. As P. Hill (1981) shows with the Federated Learning Communities program at the State University of New York at Stony Brook, with some imagination and effort, distribution courses can be used as raw material for an educationally valuable type of general education for some students, in spite of their individual limitations.

The central issues raised by a core course are the same whether it is sponsored by the college or by an academic division. Even if one were to accept the educational sufficiency of the liberal culture form of liberal education for a core course, its coverage rationale requires some deliberate decisions about what material must be "acquired" in order to be a well-educated person. Since no general education course can be fully comprehensive, what are the principles of selection?

Even if one were to accept the "Western tradition" as a sufficient source of material from which the core course were to be constructed, it must be realized that this is not a homogeneous, static tradition. It is a rich, multi ethnic cultural and social legacy that has been subjected to profound influences from all parts and peoples of the globe and continues to evolve and change over time and by place. Selection cannot be avoided and remains central to the enterprise. There are no correct decisions, but there are a vast number of wrong ones. In addition, it is unlikely that any particular set of decisions will be appropriate for more than a few years. As changes occur in the faculty, student body, and broader context in which an institution exists, it is hard to imagine that what is considered to be important to teach and for students to learn at one time will be usefully regarded as a timeless, frozen set of information, books, or whatever.

The syllabus of each general education core course should be debated frequently and widely, in order for it to serve as a vehicle for faculty development and for developing institutional identity. If these debates are not well structured, of course, they can easily become vehicles for faculty regression and institutional disintegration. In any case, engaging in the process and arriving at successive approximations of a defensible general education program are clearly important components of faculty responsibilities, even though such responsibilities are not accorded a very high priority by the tenets of disciplinary professionalism.

These observations about general education, however, accept the coverage rationale of the current general education debate, and that is a mistake. If the intellectual questions considered to be of significance and worthy of interpretation are not deliberately incorporated into the program's design and teaching, the result will be a set of intellectually impoverished courses that tend to collapse into a positivist form of liberal culture and cheat the students. If the courses are not carefully constructed so as to have meaning for students, they will fail from the formidable market pressure that students can exert. For better or for worse, college and university students are not as deferential in front of authority, alive or dead, as they were 30 years ago. Many are unwilling to study Shakespeare and Marx because the faculty say that it is good for them, that it is necessary in order to join the discourse of educated people (the cocktail party rationale). Without the meaning, there is little chance that the students will actively engage these writings and the issues they raise. The educational result of a program in which the intellectually substantive goals of general education are supplanted by a tour around a "body of knowledge" is that students are presented with a series of exhumed cadavers rather than vibrant ideas capable of significantly affecting their thinking and, indeed, their ability to think.

I will return to the subject of general education in Chapter 4.

BEYOND COVERAGE

With core courses and distribution requirements based on inert rationales of coverage, the idea of liberal education survives mainly as a vaguely defined artifact in faculty (and, increasingly, popular) culture. In the main event, undergraduate major curricula in liberal arts disciplines are diluted versions of graduate professional programs designed to train research professionals, and the differences between the liberal arts and programs in education, business, engineering, and whatever (the B.A. versus the B.S. and other specialized baccalaureates) primarily reflect the historical roots of the subject matter, an atavistic form of elitism, and conventions of administrative organization, rather than distinctive educational conceptions and practices.

Apart from some courses that explicitly focus on epistemological issues and those that stress subjective or creative elements, the stance toward knowledge in liberal arts courses and professional courses is, for all intents and purposes, indistinguishable. Dedication to the idea of positive knowledge remains the central premise of curricular design (even if not of research), and knowledge is considered to be an inert, objectified mass external to the student. The teaching function, therefore, is seen to be the transmission of this mass—whether the subject is ancient history or modern management techniques—into the students.

Efforts in the liberal culture dimension, whether known as general education, breadth, or whatever, need to be pursued vigorously, but they should not be allowed to constitute the exclusive definition of general education purposes. The criticism in the last couple of paragraphs suggests the need to revive, in an appropriately modified form, the second historical strand of liberal education goals: mental discipline as the means of development of intellectual capacities. This strand, shorn of the language of mental faculties from eighteenth- and nineteenth-century psychology, still survives in the fulsome rhetoric of college catalogues, where the goals of liberal education invariably include something along the lines of "the promotion of critical, independent thinking."

The reassertion of intellectual capabilities as a direct part of liberal education is consistent with current reassessments and critiques of positivism. Just as in the nineteenth century, when the sciences led epistemological thinking by providing the paradigm of positive knowledge, so in the twentieth century the sciences and mathematics have influenced epistemology by questioning that positive conception of knowledge. Statistical laws, wave/particle duality, the principle of uncertainty, relativity theory, quantum mechanics, and the incompleteness theorem have all stressed and finally crumbled the ideal of a unitary, fully knowable physical reality external to human perception and aspiration (Cassirer, 1950; Toulmin & Goodfield, 1962).

Parallel to the late-nineteenth- and early-twentieth-century exploration of the foundations of physical theory, pioneers in the sociology of knowledge developed an analysis of the practical, political, and economic dimensions of the creation of knowledge and of the organization of knowledge workers into professions (e.g., Mannheim, 1936). This vision has spread so widely that it would be difficult to find a field that lacks some level of reflective awareness about its organization, implicit values, status as a disciplinary profession, and socioeconomic ramifications.

In addition, one of the legacies of the 1960s in U.S. higher education is the significant presence of interestingly heterodox scholars and scholarship, which has opened up both the subject matters and methods of academic disciplines and consequently has reduced the parochialism of disciplinary professionalism. So while the new scholarship has not seriously challenged the importance of disciplinary categories, it has made the mainstream of disciplinary scholarship a much broader and more varied current. It is surprising that, while this new scholarship has affected individual courses and occasionally been the basis of a new program in, say, women's studies, the approaches to knowledge contained in the scholarship have had very little influence on general practice of college and university teaching and the undergraduate curriculum.

Academics rarely apply their sophisticated sense of their own disciplines to discussions of undergraduate curricula. So long as colleges and universities continue to evaluate curricula in such terms as essential knowledge, completeness of coverage, or ideal balances between breadth and depth, they reveal their commitment to positivistic assumptions. Educational principles and practices are not usefully guided by such notions, all of which regard knowledge as a given terrain, capable of being surveyed and then colonized for specialized exploration.

On the other hand, if one takes knowledge to be socially constructed, dependent on interpretation, and requiring a context of values to give it meaning, it follows that the central goal of undergraduate liberal education is for students to develop habits of conscious, disciplined, and informed reflection, and not merely to acquire and repeat particular bodies of information and method. This conception of liberal education requires students to recognize that questions asked by scholars come from sources other than some inherent, putatively universal qualities of knowledge structures, and that while propositions should have empirical referents, a range of defensible inferences is often consistent with the same evidence.

Aptly expressing the educational significance of this epistemological position, Hutchins (1968) wrote, "The mind is not a receptacle; information is not education. Education is what remains after the information that has been taught has been forgotten. Ideas, methods, habits of mind are the radioactive deposits left by education" (p. 38). One can admire this quotation, whether or not one agrees with the curricular conclusions Hutchins drew from it.

In this discussion, I am definitely not arguing a naive relativism that sees all knowledge to be essentially subjective. This type of radical individualism has its advocates, of course, just as it did in the epistemological debates of early-nineteenth-century Germany. But is has fewer advocates now in the United States than it did in the especially self-absorptive, me-oriented strand of the cultural ferment in the late 1960s and early 1970s (Lasch, 1968).

Between the poles of positivism and subjectivism is a rather modest and comfortable middle ground that is not at all foreign to the actual practice of most contemporary U.S. scholarship, but that still would have profound pedagogical consequences if taken seriously in college and university classrooms. This position is concisely and cogently expressed in Hekman's (1983) study of Max Weber:

> Along with the neo–Kantians, Weber defines reality as an "infinite flux" which cannot be apprehended in its totality. He assumes, further, that all knowledge is abstraction from the concreteness of reality; in other words, that "knowing" anything about this infinite flux means removing (abstracting) particular elements from the concretely real. A corollary of this neo–Kantian position, to which Weber also subscribed, is that no knowledge is possible without conceptualization, because concepts are the means by which abstraction from the concreteness of reality is effected. [p. 20]

While this view of knowledge means that attention to the effective and responsible use of empirical evidence is a definite part of the educational agenda, it maintains that knowledge does not exist without prior conceptualization and that the creation and constitution of meaning more aptly describes the process both by which human knowledge is expanded and by which individuals learn.

This thinking is consistent with much of the most interesting and growing currents of research scholarship, perhaps most notably symbolic anthropology, desconstructionist approaches in literature, and feminist scholarship in a variety of fields. While some of this work verges on a subjectivity of radical individualism that conveniently depoliticizes the scholarly enterprise, such attention to the construction of knowledge and meaning is exciting and would be very fruitful if applied in a systematic way to the curriculum and to classroom teaching.

These nonpositivist conceptions of the character of knowledge have very definite implications for instruction, because it means that teaching strategies should pay close attention to the character of analytical frameworks, including the significance of their underlying premises and selectivity, and to the complexity of interrelationships in order to succeed in getting students to appreciate the power, usefulness, and limitations of abstraction and the need for it to be used appropriately.

It is both crucial and difficult to teach students the power and limitations of abstraction and causal analytical frameworks. But getting students to accept a particular set of unexamined and often unstated assumptions and precepts is a far cry from teaching them the ways in which the focus of a theory defines the range of issues considered and questions asked, circumscribes the range of acceptable answers, and sets the terms in which they may be debated. Abstraction and analytical tools must be used deliberately and self-consciously, and it is absolutely essential that curricula engage students, actively and critically, in the interpretation of knowledge.

By conducting undergraduate education so as to stress active, critical intellectual engagement, liberal education has a considerably better chance of being truly liberating in a way that supports a broader democratic vision. But this type of education is, by its very nature, subversive and can easily cause the institution to become a target of serious criticism. John Dewey was fully cognizant of the subversive ("progressive"?) nature of education that stimulates critical thinking, and Lawrence Cremin (1961) quotes him as saying,

> If we once start thinking, no one can guarantee what will be the outcome, except that many objects, ends and institutions will be surely doomed.

Every thinker puts some portion of an apparently stable world in peril, and no one can wholly predict what will emerge in its place. [p. 350]

It is not the safe path, and the academic recession in the last couple of decades reminds us how vulnerable are the institutions, and the posture of the institutions reminds us how timid are academics and academic administrators. Such an approach to teaching requires considerable integrity as well as sincere efforts to educate those outside the academy. It will not be immediately clear to everyone why so much of what goes on in the classroom seems to involve questioning accepted social and political practices or may appear contrary to public aesthetic tastes. It is education of this type that requires academic freedom and underlies the educational reason for faculty tenure. That is, this is a reason that stems from the fundamental character of the educational enterprise rather than from a smug profession's desire for guildlike security (Cadwallader, 1983).

This understanding of knowledge and education also supplies an extremely useful criterion for understanding the major differences among various courses and programs of studies. Instead of the principal criterion for such sorting being liberal arts versus professional curricula, based on extremely vague and inconsistent notions of subject matter and method, the more fruitful distinction is the way various courses and programs *approach* knowledge. By this notion, liberal education does not stand in contrast to professional education, but rather to "training," a style of learning in which knowledge is considered to be inert and external to the student and teacher. In the training mode of education, the teacher transmits a body of information and techniques to students and judges their abilities to reproduce and apply it following prescribed procedures. It is not difficult to recognize courses that have training as their principal objective; such courses are defined in terms of "covering" a particular subject matter, and students are expected to come up with the same answers to assigned questions and problems.

On the other hand, the type of liberal education being advocated here entails a very different approach to knowledge. According to these principles, liberal education must be seen to be an educational endeavor that regards knowledge as multifaceted and as requiring interpretation. In this, then, the role of the teacher is to develop students' abilities to use logic, evidence, and sense of context to identify the role of selection, premises, and perspectives in other people's analyses and to construct and defend interpretations of their own. In other words, students must engage self-consciously and critically in the constitution of meaning. Teaching of this type is much more an intellectual enterprise than a packaging and distributing function; the view that knowledge is (or rather ought to be) created in the course of teaching challenges the conventional idea that teaching is but the transmission of knowledge, while research, the higher-order activity, is where knowledge is discovered (e.g., Trow, 1984–1985).

In all of this, however, it needs to be acknowledged that some training is necessary for liberal education, whether as part of a general education program acquainting students with a broad array of information or as part of a specialized major program. Each program of studies, and often a single course, requires both types of learning, but in a curriculum that emphasizes critical approaches to knowledge, both faculty and students must recognize that the training component is only a vehicle for broader educational purposes.

To take one important example, is the study of foreign language a matter of training, or is it liberal education? As should be evident from the argument I have developed here, the answer depends on how language is taught. If foreign language courses are taught primarily through drill, memorization, and mechanical exercises that focus exclusively on one language, then it is training, although perhaps educationally valuable training. On the other hand, if foreign language courses include, say, strong elements of linguistics and issues about the character and significance of language in general, there is no question that these courses could definitely be full-fledged liberal education for the students.

When one looks at curricula with the training-versus-liberal-education distinctions in mind, it is clear that the liberal arts and professional labels are not the ones of primary importance. Any subject in the liberal arts, including Greek philosophy and the calculus, is fully capable of being taught as training, thereby encouraging the same unfortunate habits of mind as the worst caricature of a professional course. And the liberal arts do not hold a monopoly of subject matter appropriate for liberal education; accounting and elementary education are fully capable of being taught in ways that promote the development of students' critical intellects.

One final word about curricula that focus exclusively on the training side of education: This type of teaching lends itself readily to standardization and to being routinized. As such, it is susceptible to close supervision and monitoring by bureaucratic management—and to being conducted by electronic information processors. Neither the control nor the supplanting of people by machines is feasible in the case of research and scholarship, and the type of creative teaching necessary for what I have described as liberal education is also resistant to both. This should be taken as a cautionary tale, but the primary argument remains in the realm of pedagogy and education.

I illustrate the way in which a "professional" subject matter lends itself to liberal education in Chapter 6, on teacher education. First, though, I discuss in the next chapter the curricular principles that promote what I call an inquiry-based liberal education, with a level of detail too seldom included in the advocacy of such educational goals.

4

Principles of a Critical-Inquiry Curriculum

The conception of liberal education developed in the previous chapter is closely allied with the notion of inquiry-based or critical-inquiry education, which has rapidly gained recognition in higher education thinking during the last decade or so.[1] In order to avoid introducing new nomenclature into an area of discussion that already suffers from too much labeling, I will adopt *critical-inquiry education* as the name for my position. It must be kept in mind, however, that those who use this, or the term *inquiry education*, although sharing a common general understanding of its use, frequently differ significantly over its precise meaning. Moreover, its proponents are often extremely vague about what this notion of educational purpose presupposes in epistemological terms or implies for the organization of curricula and of faculty work.

While the inquiry definition of liberal education does bear some similarity to the mental discipline goals of the classical curriculum, especially in its reliance on the so-called transfer of training (i.e., the ability to apply the habits of mind learned in one area of inquiry to another area), it does not depend on an archaic psychology of mental faculties. A direct descendant of the mental faculties view is the mini-movement in critical thinking, which sees critical thinking as a skill that can be acquired in the abstract, detached from actual issues and analyses. As a consequence, there are textbooks that present critical thinking as a formalized technique capable of being learned by rote and applied mechanically.[2]

It should be clear that this is a far cry from what I mean by critical inquiry; mental exercises, rules of argumentation, and puzzles do not constitute an adequate pedagogy. Student study programs of the inquiry type must involve sustained study of coherently structured sets of substantive questions, dealing with clearly defined content. These questions have to address material sufficiently complex to allow for cumulatively more sophisticated treatments at various levels of analysis and for a variety of alternative insights that are significant to undergraduate students. Inquiry curricula have to contain considerable information and methodological instruction that serve as bases for liberal education.

CRITICAL INQUIRY IN THE LOWER DIVISION

There is a significant component of training in general education. Names, dates, events, and titles are among the information that undergraduates are expected to retain as part of their learning about the world and about themselves in that world. This is the standard claim made for general education, and this liberal culture aspect of the coverage rationale has expanded to the point that it virtually constitutes the whole of thinking about liberal education and general education. This does not mean that this side of liberal education is unimportant, and it is imperative that "what all students should know" be a matter of continuing consideration and debate by the faculty, who must take clear responsibility for such choices rather than abdicating them to tradition, textbook publishers, or expediency in regard to the pressures of institutional politics or the market.

As I suggest in Chapter 3, even this limited coverage goal is jeopardized if the pedagogy is directed exclusively at training. It must include what I have designated the liberal education approach—carefully planned efforts to impart significance and meaning to these pieces of information and to demonstrate the interpretive questions and process of selection, perhaps by stressing scholarly debates about their meaning. Lacking this, the whole enterprise has dubious prospects of success, even in the least ambitious, flattened terms of educational purposes as defined by a list.

Very much the same analysis is germane for recent and commendable efforts to "internationalize" curricula. There is indeed some basic information about the world that students should acquire (or have reinforced) in their undergraduate studies, but the effort should go beyond map tests, tenets of world religions, and descriptions of some exotic political and cultural practices. For example, comparative study is an excellent way for students to understand the limits of generalizations in social and cultural theory, which usually are based on rather narrow and parochial sources. Incorporating the experiences of people outside the usual purview of Anglo–American scholarship gives a new angle of vision on any number of issues that too easily can be perceived to be of strictly local significance. Again, the same principles of combining information into analytical and intellectually challenging frameworks that holds for general education is true in this specific aspect of it.

Basic skills are another special and important dimension of lower-division education. While it is imperative that the students' acquisition of basic skills such as writing and quantitative facilities not be confused and conflated with the goals of general education (as they so frequently are), the teaching of basic skills should be integrated into substantively oriented general education courses. Even remedial courses that are specifically for increasing students' abilities to express themselves in writing and to use numerical information at levels appropriate for college and university education also need to be strongly oriented to substantive issues, although most of students' and teachers' time will be devoted to improving students' skills.

By teaching skills through courses focused on substantive questions capable of engaging students, remedial courses become intrinsically more worthwhile for students and immediately demonstrate to them the tangible benefits of better expository writing skills and facility with numerical data. Examples of such courses in writing are easy to find and range across a wide spectrum of material. The distribution of income is one example of a focus capable of providing an interesting and fruitful substantive basis for quantitative courses. In institutions that do not currently grant credit for any remedial courses, partial credit could be justified for content-based ones, and that credit could be used toward the distribution requirement. Such a device would reduce the stigma while enhancing the effectiveness of remedial education.

While there is no serious debate about the importance of writing and tabulation skills for college and university students, there is some problem with regarding writing as a skill that is adequately developed by students' demonstrating a minimum competence early in their college work. Writing is an integral part of thinking, and the capacity to organize and express one's thoughts on paper (and disk) should be developed throughout the college years. Such programs as writing across the curriculum, therefore, are important beyond some idea of skills. In one effective and relatively straightforward version of this, students are required to take at least one intensive writing course each year or perhaps even each semester throughout their undergraduate years. These courses, which are designated from existing offerings in each department, are not specifically writing courses. They are regular departmental courses that assign considerable writing and are taught by departmental faculty who are literate enough to give some suggestions on exposition, in addition to dealing with the essays' contents.

Bibliographic and information-retrieval skills are another important area. This type of skill is not discussed as often in the higher education literature, but if we are serious about our students' becoming capable independent learners, they should be able to find as well as interpret information productively in order to pursue a significant question. They must understand how information is organized in both print and electronic forms, and again, such instruction should take place in the context of exploring a substantive question that makes sense to students. As opposed to the familiar library tour or one-credit mandatory library seminar, each first-year student should take at least one course that necessitates independent use of the library, with bibliographic instruction integrated into the course and directly supporting its assignments (Selin, 1988).

Such skills are necessary not only for future research as academics but also for full citizenship in our information-laden society. It is vitally important that students appreciate the power that access to and the manipulation of information entails. That is, they should be able to defend themselves against others' use of information and be alert to potential dangers stemming from restrictions on access to it.

Various types of training clearly are vital in undergraduate education, but whether that training involves learning the date of the French Revolution or acquiring a basic skill, students should not see it as an end in itself. The broader and substantive purposes of such learning must be clear to the student and the instructor alike, and the courses must be informed by the understanding that no information is neutral and that selection, categorization, and imputation of causality are all outgrowths of interpretations that embody very definite ideas about how the world goes around.

This is precisely where the most serious lapses occur, even in the best of writings about values education (e.g., Morrill, 1980). Most of the arguments for the need to incorporate values into curricula proceed on the positivist assumption that the knowledge taught in colleges and universities is value free, so some consideration of ("correct?") values needs to be injected into the education. There is indeed a cogent case to be made for explicitly introducing values issues into the curriculum, but the effort will be severely impaired if such efforts continue to be informed by the assumption that values are not already firmly embedded in the character of existing knowledge. Whether or not an institution feels it can and should articulate a clear set of values, there is absolutely no question that students must be conscious about the nature of values and about the value-laden ideology of, say, "value-free" social science, in order to have any hope of achieving critical-

inquiry goals for undergraduate education. This type of values education is crucial for liberal education, and, again, it is best accomplished
through serious study of real substance.

CRITICAL INQUIRY IN THE UPPER DIVISION

While the liberal culture and coverage conceptions of education have
expanded so that they now encompass all of general education, the
conception of liberal education has contracted to the point that it is
frequently identified exclusively with general education and, thereby,
the lower division. The critical-inquiry approach to teaching and
learning, however, insists that liberal education be an integral part of
all curricula, regardless of the subject matter and of the level at which
it is taught.

When we consider academic programs for advanced undergraduates, we have to take a closer look at the role of disciplines in the
curriculum. In Chapter 1, I emphasize the professional character of the
academic disciplines; by keeping this quality in mind, we can avoid
much of the confusion that typically accompanies such discussions
when disciplines are considered to be genuine intellectual categories.
This confusion is not limited to those who are proponents of the use of
academic disciplines to organize undergraduate education.

A Critical Look at Critiques of Disciplines

One major source of confusion is the chronic tendency of even
critics of disciplinary undergraduate education to reify disciplines as
intellectual categories. This unfortunate tendency is clear in arguments
that promote interdisciplinary work on the grounds that disciplines
overemphasize specialized rigor at the expense of breadth (e.g.,
Campbell, 1969; Hausman, 1979; Newell, 1983; Swora & Morrison,
1974).

When sociologists, historians, philosophers, anthropologists, biologists, physicists, geographers, and many, many other scholars from
different disciplines convincingly demonstrate how such a portrayal
seriously misrepresents the wide variety of legitimate work within
their disciplines, and rigor has already been conceded, the case for
interdisciplinary work is not especially compelling. Moreover, the all-
things-are-connected argument for interdisciplinary education, while
at some level obviously true, seriously distorts the intellectual and
pedagogical argument. The issue is *not* whether abstraction will be

employed, but rather which types of abstraction are the most useful to pursuing particular questions, and how conscious (and accurate) students are in selecting appropriate levels of abstraction and in acknowledging the implications of their choices.

Moreover, arguments for interdisciplinary curricula based on coverage imply the same pedagogical stance as disciplinary curricula: The teacher is the authority who will reveal knowledge. While this can be convenient (although boring) for teachers, it promotes unfortunate habits of mind among students, who too easily accept their prescribed role as passive consumers of knowledge. The stance significantly dampens the excitement, commitment, and creativity most colleges say they hope to stimulate in students.

Another problem with criticisms of disciplines predicated on the notion of coverage is that their logic unavoidably implies questioning the efficacy of disciplinary categories for research purposes, even though the critics' intentions may be limited to reforming undergraduate education. Irrespective of the merits of this questioning, the indiscriminate extension of the argument into realms about which few critics of disciplines appear either interested or capable of making cogent arguments seriously weakens their case against undergraduate disciplinary education.

By regarding academic disciplines as professions, however, one can more effectively restrict the criticism of disciplines, and at the same time avoid the awkward implications of the frequently heard charge that academic reward systems are biased in favor of research activities, at the expense of undergraduate teaching. As I argue in Chapter 1, these incentives are indeed present in disciplinary professionalism, which offers greater rewards for research and the research-oriented training of graduate students than it does for undergraduate instruction. Graduate teaching is more closely tied to faculty research, and undergraduates are much less likely to become disciplinary professionals whose subsequent careers will enhance the extra-institutional professional standing of the teacher. As a consequence, undergraduate teaching is a relatively low-status activity and not an obvious route to tangible professional benefits.

This situation is generally acknowledged, and the manner in which the academic reward system discriminates against undergraduate teaching is one of the most often criticized features of academic departments and disciplines. But, while the professional model of academic disciplines does emphasize their research character, the case does not depend on the diversion of best efforts away from undergraduate teaching. This is fortunate, because an undue emphasis on the potent effects of the incentives directing the best talent into re-search and graduate education necessarily carries with it the conclu-sion that those who are exclusively undergraduate teachers are not sufficiently smart, creative, or self-disciplined to succeed in research careers. This assessment comes from even critical commentators, who, in bemoaning the loss of quality individuals to undergraduate instruc-tion, thereby accept the disciplinary professions' definition of who the best people are (e.g., McHenry, 1977; Project on Redefining, 1985).

Tacit acceptance of conventional criteria of excellence results in an unwarranted undervaluing of the large numbers of highly talented men and women who are genuinely committed to undergraduate education and have chosen to make it the center of their careers. When one acknowledges the peculiar and self-serving nature of the disciplin-ary professions' standards of faculty merit, there is no more reason to argue that the potentially most able undergraduate teachers are di-verted away from undergraduate teaching than there is for its equally dubious converse, that those who have made it to the very top of their disciplinary professions are precisely those least suited for effective undergraduate teaching.

In addition, the empirical evidence, such as it is, consistently indicates patterns of faculty work in which teaching, and especially undergraduate teaching, is the activity to which most faculty devote by far the greatest amount of time and effort, irrespective of institu-tional type, faculty rank, gender, and discipline (Baldridge et al., 1978; Finkelstein, 1984; Shulman, 1979). The incentive system may be silly and unfair, but I am not convinced that it has, in and of itself, the serious consequences for undergraduate education that some have argued.

Critical Inquiry and the Disciplinary Curriculum

Independent of relative rewards, the overwhelming proportion of faculty committed to teaching undergraduates do their teaching in disciplinary curricula. Academic disciplines simply were not deve-loped to help undergraduates organize their thinking about the world, and there is certainly nothing in their constitution to suggest that pedagogical usefulness has been an unexpected byproduct. Yet, under-graduate liberal arts curricula continue to look like watered-down versions of graduate programs designed to train research profession-als. Even in colleges where the ethos of faculty research has never been strong, undergraduates' academic work consists, by and large, of introductions to one or more disciplines.

Returning now to the place of academic disciplines in liberal education, a first step is to recognize that disciplines differ markedly in the precision of their definitions. For our purposes, it is useful to think of arraying disciplines along an axis according to the degree and specificity of disciplinary professionals' consensus about what constitutes each discipline. At one end of the array, therefore, will be those disciplines that are loose congeries of subject matters, approaches, and techniques; at the other end will be the more tightly defined entities.

As was already suggested, most disciplines will be considerably closer to the first end of the array than to the second, and it is very difficult for the more loosely defined disciplines to create curricula that enable students to proceed to increasingly more sophisticated levels of understanding along consistent lines of inquiry. The group of upper-division courses a student finally chooses to satisfy a major in one of these disciplines—most often in the humanities and social sciences—is typically diffuse in content and horizontal in trajectory. Completing major requirements in one of these disciplines is an experience that makes about as much educational sense as satisfying distribution requirements that have been fashioned by log-rolling in faculty politics.

At the other end of the array, where the more specifically defined disciplines are located, there are other problems. Here there is more clarity and specificity about what comprises the discipline, even though the wide range of applications recognized as legitimate within, say, economics and physics blurs some of the clarity. As opposed to those at the more casual end of the spectrum, the curricula of this class of disciplines are more coherent and cumulative. As a direct result of the consensus by disciplinary professionals, however, the discipline is presented to undergraduates as a category of codified subject matter and techniques. That is, these disciplines have solved basic conceptual problems (arising, for the most part, out of research), so their curricula point students in directions that have been set by those solutions and discourage questioning the intellectual grounds for those directions.

Getting students to accept a particular set of unexamined and often unstated assumptions and precepts is a far cry from teaching them the ways in which the resulting focus of a theory defines the range of issues considered and questions asked, thereby circumscribing the range of acceptable answers and setting the terms in which they may be debated. Liberal education goals require abstraction and analytical tools to be used deliberately and self-consciously, and it is absolutely essential that curricula engage students, actively and critically, in the creation and interpretation of knowledge. Curricula of well-developed disciplines, because they are so well developed, seldom explore the implications of particular disciplinary categories, and thus they tend to expose students to the *results* of thinking rather than involve them as active participants in the processes of that thought.

Some of the most serious problems along these lines might be avoided if the discipline itself were to be the subject of critical study. The anomaly of this tactic, however, is that, for it to be done well, it could not be done under the sole auspices of the particular discipline. It would require drawing heavily from intellectual and social history, philosophy, sociology of knowledge, and so on.

But in regard to the main argument, please notice its odd quality: Some disciplines are too diffuse in content to be satisfactory bases of an inquiry curriculum, while others are too tightly constructed. Not only are both these observations accurate, but *no intermediate points along the array are satisfactory either.* The argument is simply that preset, unexamined categories of knowledge, whether consistent and coherent or not, do not lend themselves to curricular forms appropriate for inquiry goals. Learning a discipline is simply not an adequate goal for liberal education.[3]

There are no conceptual or pedagogical reasons that prevent disciplinary faculty from constructing inquiry-oriented individual courses or even programs of study around subsets of disciplinary subject matters. Apart from possible professional difficulties, however, when one begins to develop undergraduate curricula around some clear questions, it is contrary to the logic of the study to restrict the scope of the inquiry to that of the sponsoring discipline. For the purposes of critical inquiry, the need is for curricula that are narrower than most disciplines in central questions and themes but at the same time are broader than most disciplines in approaches, perspectives, contexts, theoretical formulations, and techniques.

CONTENT AND PROCESS

As in many such discussions I have had, I have been using the distinctions between content and process in at least two different ways, and it is time to clarify their meanings and relationships.

Intellectual Content Versus Pedagogical Process

I will begin with the distinction between intellectual content, representing the substantive materials and inquiry being taught, and pedagogical process, as the means by which the materials and inquiry are presented to students in the classroom.[4] The best debates about the relative importance of these two dimensions of teaching have taken place in the literature on primary and secondary public schooling. My stress on the intellectual goals of undergraduate education is similar to that of the critics of progressive education in the public schools during the 1940s and 1950s.

Perhaps the best among the books in this genre was *Educational Wastelands* (1953), in which Bestor asserted that the development of students' intellectual capacities has to be seen as the primary goal of public education. He argued that progressive educators' commitment to a peculiar vision of democratic education had led them to stress pedagogical issues (e.g., "starting from where the students are") and to be suspicious of elite education to the point that they had seriously diluted the intellectual content of the curriculum. Bestor's central argument was that the best democratic education was the strongly intellectual orientation of what had been identified as aristocratic education, and that it would be democratic when it became the education for all. Anthing less ambitious in terms of content or expected outcomes, such as the progressive educators "life adjustment education," cheats the students and threatens the foundations of democratic society. More recently, Bowles and Gintis (1976) argue a similar view, from a different political perspective.

This argument is very appealing, especially when it is compared to the paucity of such thinking in the current debates about schooling in the 1980s. Such a vision of democratic education—or, for that matter, *any* vision of democratic education—is a statistically insignificant occurrence among mainstream criticisms of schooling in the 1980s. The 1983 report of the U.S. National Commission on Excellence in Education, *A Nation at Risk*, illustrates this point by its lack of any such vision. One major exception to this trend is Adler (1984), whose view of democratic education is similar to that of Bestor (1953), but superior by virtue of the imaginative pedagogy he suggests to carry it out.

The serious weakness in Bestor (1953) is that, in his vigorous fight against progressive educator's stress on pedagogy—which Cremin (1964) contends is a distortion of Dewey's educational thought—Bestor denigrates the importance of pedagogy (process) and thus seriously weakens his argument for democratic education. His inattention to *how* lofty intellectual educational goals were to be achieved makes his discussion of examinations and standards sound as though the proposed intellectual content of education would perform its historical function, as a barrier to social mobility, a screening mechanism to reproduce the structure of power and privilege.

This certainly is not what we understand democratic education to be about. Making one's case about education too exclusively in terms of either side of the duality—progressive educators' pedagogical process or Bestor's (1953) intellectual content—is inadequate and dangerous. Educational ideals must be defined in terms that explicitly acknowledge and respect the importance of the interaction of intellectual content and pedagogical process.

Curricular Content Versus Intellectual Process

The second distinction between content and process is the difference between two kinds of educational goal. The intellectual process side is the capacity for critical, rational thought, while the content side refers to the substantive questions, themes, and materials to which the intellectual processes are applied. In these terms, there is an interestingly anomalous relationship between curricular content and intellectual process in an inquiry curriculum. In advocating an ideal of critical-inquiry or liberal education that is constituted in terms of intellectual capabilities and habits of mind, I have repeatedly asserted that the content of the curriculum must be sufficiently complex and worthwhile to support these goals. In respect to intellectual process goals, therefore, the role of curricular content appears to be instrumental.

But the liberal education goal is an *institutional* goal, and the principal commitments of students and faculty are properly to the substantive questions themselves. The process of liberal education and inquiry from the vantagepoint of faculty and students, therefore, is contained in the critical approaches to the questions and stances toward answers that are seen as instrumentally necessary to pursue the substantive questions productively.

So curricular content and intellectual process are inextricably intertwined. The belief that one—content or process—needs to be chosen over the other, or even that it is possible to do so, is specious. It is obvious that discussions framed in ways that even imply that education is a matter of content versus process are not likely to be productive.

CRITICAL-INQUIRY CURRICULA

While critical-inquiry curricula need to be interdisciplinary, they are significantly different from interdisciplinary efforts informed by a coverage rationale, and their specialized nature enables them to draw effectively from disciplines without at the same time reifying them. The term *adisciplinary* rather than *interdisciplinary*, may be more appropriate. According to critical-inquiry principles, teaching undergraduate students the relations among academic disciplines makes even less sense as an educational goal than teaching students a single discipline, although the former would be worthwhile for graduate students going into college and university teaching. The purpose is to develop students' abilities to explore and understand, even in a preliminary way, the connections among ideas and natural, social, and cultural phenomena.

It is very important, then, that academic disciplines, as they are currently regarded and practiced, not comprise the exclusive organizing device of either lower- or upper-division curricula. A substantial part of a student's work should be accomplished through coherently structured curricula that are thematic or problem centered. Pedagogy in a critical-inquiry curriculum should contain certain features, and these qualities should draw strong and clear support from the curriculum's very structure and sense of purpose. That is, the whole enterprise should be conceived of and designed in such a manner that certain types of teaching modes are obvious and natural.

First of all, courses should be defined by questions rather than by coverage. This in itself contributes to a tone of open-ended inquiry that encourages students to think of new questions rather than grope for pat answers. Building on this, course formats need to include authentic opportunities for students, separately and together, to pursue questions and to construct meanings. As has already been noted in support of this, assigned tasks must develop critical, bibliographic, quantitative, and expository writing skills serving the broader goals of substantive inquiry, because a sure command of these skills is essential to students' engaging actively in the process of exploring the bases of alternative explanations, to say nothing of the demands of work and citizenship after college.

It also is extremely important for students to have the opportunity to respond to faculty comments and criticisms by revising, refining, and extending arguments in their written work, beyond their needs to learn how to write better. That is, the written expression of students' ideas and analyses should be treated as continuing intellectual efforts in an area of inquiry, rather than simply as a way to judge their performance. Revising and reworking arguments and evidence helps to replace the artificial quality of typical course requirements with a climate of intellectual responsibility. If students are expected to defend, elaborate, and further articulate their position in response to criticism, they are encouraged to take their own critical perspectives and interpretations more seriously. Requiring (or allowing) students to revise their work also fosters the idea that making mistakes is an integral part of learning. With this type of environment, students can be encouraged to take intellectual risks, a crucial component of active learning.

Another aspect of active learning and student involvement is establishing periodic points at which students clearly state and discuss the ideas and principles that guide their course selections, both retrospectively and prospectively. I have mentioned the quality of coherence a couple of times in this chapter, but what I have in mind does not necessitate the faculty's designing a curriculum that in their view has a beginning, middle, and end. The necessary coherence is in the *students'* seeing the connections among a range of courses and being able to articulate the nature of those connections, no matter how tentative the connections may be at any particular juncture. Each student should have the opportunity to reflect upon, articulate, and defend her or his choices and how they add up in respect to personal educational goals and aspirations and institutional standards.

Such an opportunity to make sense out of their course-selection patterns reduces the fragmentation that all too often typifies the undergraduate educational experience. Fifteen years ago, the Carnegie Foundation (1977) suggested that students' preferences for explicitly professional curricula may be as much a reflection of those curricula's greater coherence as of students' careerism.

Although more difficult to implement, it is desirable for students' work to have a definite cumulative quality. Although some of this may be achieved through a system of prerequisites, a study program could be cumulative if students were simply expected to draw upon their previous course learning to enrich their work in current courses. This need not entail rigid sequences of prerequisites, but, as noted, it is difficult though not impossible to achieve within the conventional course system. It entails some forum for faculty attention to the pattern of student work outside of that available by instructors in individual courses.[5]

CONCLUDING REMARKS

I am calling for definite changes, but I do not believe that achieving some of the most important goals of critical-inquiry education requires the complete transformation and rededication of the academy called for by some reformers (e.g., Martin, 1982; Project on Redefining, 1985). Thinking on a grand scale is salutary, for it does help us to rethink current organizations and practices, but there is always the suspicion that those who can call for nothing but complete revolution may lack imagination. I subscribe to the dictum that, for both tactical and strategic reasons, in U.S. colleges and universities one should engage in overall thinking but piecemeal action (Carnegie Foundation, 1978). For an example of how rather modest changes in organization and thinking might produce some substantial educational benefits, in Chapter 5 I will outline two examples of curricular revision that entail only relatively slight changes in the organization of faculty work but still hold considerable promise.

PART II

Approaches to a Liberal Education Curriculum

5

Two Examples of
Curricular Innovation

There are numerous curricular innovations that might be feasible for
many colleges and universities. The two presented in this chapter,
taken singly or together, could constitute important steps toward the
type of undergraduate education advocated in the previous chapters,
and neither entails expensive or drastic changes. They are presented
primarily as examples of curricular thinking, rather than as prescriptions.

TAKING ACADEMIC ADVISING SERIOUSLY

Declarations about the need for more effective student advising
abound in speeches, reports, articles, and books on higher education,
and there is no question about its importance or about the faculty
being the best source of academic advice for students. But even at the
most constricted level of aspiration, the quality of advising remains
weak, and there is a paucity of ideas for improving it. One problem is
that the function of academic advising is usually regarded as merely
the delivery of responsible information and advice to students. I argue
that academic advising offers a valuable device for promoting broader
and more interesting educational goals.

In order for academic advising to be a vital part of undergraduate
education, it must be integrated into the faculty's academic work in a
way that accurately reflects both its value for students and the faculty
time and effort that good advising requires. This is most easily and
feasibly done through the course-credit system, and I suggest that the
centerpiece of the academic advising system be a mandatory advising
seminar awarded one credit each term.

In this scheme, individual faculty advisers would meet with each
class (e.g., freshmen, juniors) of their advisees for, say, a couple of
hours every second week to discuss the assigned seminar readings. For

lower-division advising seminars, the syllabus would be the same throughout the institution and organized around questions that are appropriate for the particular mission and students. Two examples are, "What is an educated person?" and, "What is liberal education, and is it good for you?"

Irrespective of how the seminars might be framed, they could productively include materials on the historical development of U.S. higher education, on the rationales for distinguishing among different realms of knowledge, and on research concerning the effects of higher education on students. In this last area, for example, I have found that students respond quite enthusiastically to Perry's (1981) work on student cognitive development, which has led me to take the article more seriously. Finally, the only written assignment would be for the students to reflect on their own past and future study programs, drawing *critically* from the readings and seminar discussions.

In the comprehensive, eight-semester model, faculty advisers would be drawn from upper-division students' major department, and the advising seminars' syllabi would be common for the department. In the case of liberal arts majors, the seminars could give students the opportunity to read about the origins of the academic discipline and to debate a range of critical works on the nature and definition of the discipline. The departmental syllabi for students majoring in professional programs could focus on the relationship between the academy and that profession and between liberal education and professional education. For majors in both liberal arts and professional programs, the final paper for each semester's seminar, again, would be an analysis of the student's own study program—upper division and lower division, requirements and electives—in light of a critical understanding of the issues involved.

I have described an advising system that presupposes a certain type of college or university. It is clear that it would have to be modified, perhaps significantly, for places where institutional organization and the student body do not conform to the assumptions behind my sketch.[1] Even when the assumptions are accurate, however, the logistics would not be simple. It would behoove faculty to have advisees in no more than two class cohorts, perhaps freshmen and juniors or sophomores and seniors, so that they had only two advising seminars a term. The advising seminar would have to be within the regular teaching load, otherwise the whole idea is simply another form of speed-up for faculty, who, contrary to the impression one can get from some of the writings on higher education (e.g., Cahn, 1986;

Project on Redefining, 1985), are generally hard working and dedicated.

Before getting mired down in the difficulties, however, it is important to review the definite advantages of such a scheme. The seminars would be a forum for systematically informing students about the nature of the educational enterprise, thus allowing them to acquire a better perspective on that enterprise. For example, such an informed perspective would help to remedy the chronic inadequacy of colleges' and universities' explaining the reasons for general education requirements, which all too easily can appear to students to be simply meaningless hurdles.

Some structurally integrated effort is necessary if students are to be able to think knowledgeably about their college education, and this effort should be in the context of their active involvement in planning and reconsidering their own programs of study throughout their student years. Students need to understand how their diverse learning experiences can and should constitute a coherent education. The faculty can design curricula that are logically integrated and beautifully consistent, but, if the principles underlying the design are obscure to those being educated, the students most likely will perceive their college education as a series of fragmented experiences.

With advising seminars, not only would students' individual conversations with their faculty advisers be more useful, but students would have a common educational experience. The value of this commonality would be enhanced by the fact that the seminars expressed the distinctive character of the individual college or university as well as had a cumulative character. These properties are woefully scarce, especially in social science and humanities curricula.

There are definite advantages for faculty in such a scheme. For instance, the seminars and the resulting essays would constitute a definite and developing context that would clarify how their one-to-one conversations with advisees should be structured. The faculty should also find that the seminar readings help them to locate their work and institution more firmly in the order of things. Moreover, the faculty side of the students' "common educational experience" can become a means for faculty in the same and other departments to develop more in the way of shared vocabulary and premises for talking about undergraduate education. At the very least, a humanist and a scientist could productively combine and jointly teach their advising seminars when certain problematic issues are raised by the readings.

Finally, a system of advising seminars would be an explicit statement that faculty advising really is highly valued and not merely a vaguely defined extra that needs constant exhortations to work even sporadically well. Advising would be explicitly incorporated into the calculus of faculty work by counting tangibly in the arithmetic competition among faculty and departments. Perhaps the freshman advising seminar should be given two credit hours, reflecting its greater importance and difficulty; and, if faculty in departments with few majors were given disproportionate numbers of new student advisees, teaching loads would be somewhat evened out. Moreover, by the use of seminars, the advising function could legitimately be evaluated as a dimension of teaching, which is precisely how it should be regarded.

Academic advising should be supplemented by personal counseling, career advising, and other kinds of support. Although it is not useful to exaggerate such distinctions in dealing with an individual, these other types of advising still should not be confused with the more purely academic side of course and program selection that is fundamentally educational and thus should primarily be the responsibility of the faculty. The academic facet of advising should be taken more seriously as a crucial *educational* endeavor and therefore conducted in a manner parallel to other educational endeavors, and integrating it with the course system would be a good start in this direction.

THEMATIC MINOR PROGRAMS OF STUDY

The second example of curricular innovation centers on the use of minor programs of study. Minor programs seem to be making a comeback in liberal arts colleges and divisions, and, although this change has not been as dramatic as the resurgence of general education requirements, it is a significant aspect of colleges' and universities' widespread movement toward prescription and structure. Such momentum could be built upon to affect the character and potentials of liberal education by requiring students to enroll in a thematic minor program in addition to a major.

While most minors are disciplinary minors, which are simply abbreviated versions of major programs, I am advocating the development of an array of thematic minors, each organized around a set of substantive questions dealing with a clearly defined content area. It is easy to suggest suitable subject matter from which such questions could be constructed: urban problems; environmental issues; area studies (e.g., Africa, Asia, Latin America, Soviet Union, and so on);

patterns and significance of technological change; the experiences of blacks and of women in the United States; international relations (perhaps with an emphasis on national security and disarmament); a regional studies program drawing on local resources; children (including nature-versus-nurture debates, the varieties and meanings of youth cultures); the "graying" of America; energy (sources and uses); the place of religion in private and public life; high culture, popular culture, and the media; and so on. The choices would depend on student and faculty interests and on institutional resources.

The curriculum for these programs need not be elaborate; a lower-division course and a four-course upper-division sequence would be sufficient. The individual upper-division courses would not have to be interdisciplinary, but it *is* critical from the very beginning that each course explicitly address the respective programs' common questions, albeit from different perspectives; that each course deliberately and consistently refer to and build upon the materials of the preceding courses in the sequence; and that each entail explicit explorations of the implications of abstraction and particular categories of knowledge.

The main purpose of establishing such a system of minors is to structure a part of the curriculum along the lines of critical inquiry. Even alongside disciplinary majors, there is good reason to believe that this relatively modest change would make an educational difference. By supplying students with a consistent line of inquiry to which they have a definite commitment, a minor can increase the coherence and meaning of disciplinary majors by giving students a consistent substantive strand to which they can relate their major courses. By its structure, the minor program of study would confirm (or more likely begin to impart) a cumulative, progressive character to their studies not common in disciplinary majors, where, especially in the humanities and social sciences, student programs are all too often diffuse in content and essentially horizontal in trajectory.

In addition to its support of the principal argument about critical-inquiry education, there are five further advantages to be derived from instituting a system of minors like those described here. These are advantages that flow from the thematic, interdisciplinary character of the minors, but are in themselves sufficiently significant and tangible that many faculty may find these additional aspects to be more persuasive than arguments based on general convictions about inquiry or interdisciplinary education.

General education. A system of thematic minors would supply the organizational mechanism, and the minors' specialized focus would form the intellectual contexts, for systematically extending general education into the upper-division years. Analyses from the humanities, sciences, and social sciences could easily be incorporated into most (and perhaps all) of the themes, and completion of such a minor could therefore count toward satisfying distribution requirements. By being able to choose among a range of minor programs, each of which progressed to increasingly sophisticated levels, students would be far less likely to perceive (and experience) general education as comprised of arbitrary hurdles of little intrinsic interest and intellectual challenge. Furthermore, these very same qualities should evoke more commitment from faculty than general education efforts limited to the level of introductory surveys. Finally, by taking some of the general education burden out of the lower-division years, it should be easier to articulate curricula of four-year institutions with those of community colleges, thus easing a student's transition from one type of institution to the other.

Specific educational purposes. The flexibility of the minors would allow them to be developed for particular sets of students. For instance, some minor programs could be tailored, say, to serve an honors program or to promote the sustained development of writing and quantitative skills. Others could be designed especially for students majoring in professional programs. The case for professional students' taking a substantial number of liberal arts courses simply is not very convincing when it is based primarily on vague, unsupported, and ultimately suspect claims about qualities of liberal education that all liberal arts courses (and only liberal arts courses) putatively embody. But well-organized packages of thematic minors directed to particular groups of professional students (e.g., Business in American Thought; Politics of Schooling) could be considerably more attractive to colleagues and students in professional curricula.

Moreover, if liberal arts divisions provided coherent sets of liberal education courses that complemented professional curricula in clearly valuable ways, professional programs might be more amenable to offering minors for liberal arts students, assuaging students' and parents' anxieties about employment prospects.

Program development. A system of thematic minors would allow an institution to give meaningful curricular expression to areas that represent strong faculty and student commitments (e.g., black studies, women's studies) but have trouble sustaining themselves as full departments competing with conventional disciplinary departments. Thematic minors may thus be a means for an authentic curricular pluralism that would create more space for different educational and political visions and reduce competition among internal factions.

Institutional identity. Related to the third point, the range of feasible minor programs would be determined by faculty and student interests and institutional resources and mission. But these factors are not merely constraints; they insure that the actual configuration of minor programs will express the special and distinctive character of a liberal arts college or division with a vividness not available through disciplinary majors. The striking similarity of liberal arts major programs in virtually every institution has flattened out the diversity of U.S. higher education and, by doing so, has created the conditions for measures of "quality" to be the principal (and often exclusive) criterion for differentiating among liberal arts programs. (This is treated in more detail in Chapter 12.)

This one-dimensional mode of comparison is, in my opinion, undesirable both because measures of quality are essentially just measures of relative privilege and because uniform conceptions of quality actively promote even greater institutional conformity. Establishing a system of thematic minor programs, therefore, may constitute a substantial break with current pressures for greater upper-division curricular homogeneity.

A college's or university's curriculum sets the range of student choice and encourages particular student attitudes toward learning. Through the catalogue, the curriculum becomes a public, operational statement of what the institution considers to be educationally important. The importance of the curriculum as a declaration of institutional identity should not be underestimated.

Faculty development. Thematic minors could serve as important forums of faculty professional growth. Minor programs would engage faculty across disciplines, but on specialized questions of interest, and the type of intellectual stimulation from working with new sets of colleagues to design upper-division thematic minors is particularly important when there are low rates of faculty turnover and reduced opportunities for professional advancement and mobility. If the faculty are going to be able to sustain the intellectual vitality and commitment necessary for first-rate scholarship and teaching, the curriculum is simply going to have to be rewarding and educational for faculty as well as for students.

In respect to improving teaching, it is frequently argued that tinkering with curricula is less important for educational quality than are faculty ability and dedication (e.g., Veysey, 1973). Excellent teachers can indeed give students first-rate educations in standard, uninspired curricula, but they do so in spite of those curricula and the pressures (and temptations) of disciplinary categories and professionalism. Qualities such as responsibility, goodwill, and shared commitment are vitally important, but they must be nurtured and supported by the institutional framework in which teaching is done.

The assertion that excellent teaching is *the* critical factor in excellent undergraduate education has the attractiveness of all tautologies, but the argument tends to be static in nature, implying that effective teachers are born, not developed. As such, it fits comfortably into the ideology of disciplinary professionalism and the reluctance to consider teaching as a genuine part of professional work and development (see Mauksch, 1980, for a similar argument). When one accepts the possibility of increasing pedagogical effectiveness, however, it follows that a curriculum that is exciting and educational for teachers is a surer path to excellent teaching than one that expresses an immutable, inherited codification of knowledge structures.

I discuss further the significance of faculty intellectual development in later chapters, but here it is necessary to note how these potential benefits compare with the expected costs of establishing and operating a system of minor programs. The cost side of the ledger is not especially daunting. First of all, this curricular improvement can be achieved without challenging disciplinary departments' hegemony over major programs. This means that departments can be retained for their value as a brake on administrative authority and as a locus for decisions about personnel and research that can be made according to previously established and relatively clear standards. The educational resources necessary for such a system of minor programs could come chiefly from reallocation rather than from augmentation, which could be directed along lines that would systematically tighten up major curricula plagued by course proliferation and would even up enrollments among fields.

The political costs involved in establishing the programs of minors need not be prohibitive. The proposal has a somewhat traditional ring to it and would entail only a modest rearrangement of curricular organization and faculty work, as opposed to the relatively breathtaking "rededication of the academy" so often blithely proposed. The introduction of the minor system would require collective faculty agreement at only quite general levels of educational purpose and structure, and small groups of faculty, presumably with long-standing commitments to particular subject matters, would work out the specifics of individual minor programs. If framed intelligently, then, such a proposal should not be perceived as being terribly threatening by even the most beleaguered and defensive segments of the liberal arts faculty (although one cannot afford to be too sanguine about this).

Finally, while each program no doubt would quickly begin to operate as an interest group in faculty politics, the life cycle of any one minor or even of the whole pattern is capable of being decided with considerable freedom. This is not so in the case of disciplinary majors and departments, which are key units of faculty professional life within the institution and derive much of their definition and legitimacy from outside the institution. That is, the ease with which a particular minor could be abolished for reasons of student undersubscription, faculty interest, or whatever, is a type of flexibility that is unusual and highly desirable in current academic offerings.

6

Teacher Education,
Liberal Education,
and the Liberal Arts

It is a firmly established tenet, accepted by many teacher educators, that liberal arts curricula are more intellectually demanding and worthwhile than are teacher education (or other "professional") programs. An obvious conclusion from this assessment is that, in the effort to upgrade teacher education programs, more liberal arts instruction should be incorporated into them (e.g., Carbone, 1980; Commission for Educational Quality, 1985; Ducharme, 1980; Herson, 1980; Holmes Group, 1986; Rich, 1980; U.S. National Commission, 1983).

Those defending teacher education programs frequently respond to this prescription by pointing out that many and often most upper-division courses taken by students pursuing careers in secondary education are in liberal arts departments, and large proportions of all teacher preparation programs already entail substantial numbers of lower- and upper-division liberal arts courses. Although this response is a necessary corrective to what often is ill-informed criticism, it is seriously limited by its defensiveness and, more important, tacitly accepts the critics' terms by not challenging the presumption that education programs are inherently inferior with respect to the liberal arts. This does not, on the face of it, appear to be a very productive line of argument.

Teacher education programs do need to be strengthened considerably, and of course liberal arts programs also are in dire need of rethinking and rededication. The need to attend to teacher education programs, however, is more pressing, because colleges' and universities' granting of teaching certificates has considerably more consequence for the future of our society than does the granting of B.A. degrees. This is because of both the importance of teachers' work with students and the conditions of employment for teachers, which appears to be more protected from continuing assessments of competency than the vast majority of other occupations at which college and university graduates work. This difference can be exaggerated, but the unusual employment conditions are still sufficiently special that they put particular responsibilities on the initial certification that makes primary and secondary school teachers employable in school systems.

LIBERAL EDUCATION AND THE LIBERAL ARTS

Efforts to improve the quality of our teacher preparation programs will be severely impaired unless we clarify the relationships among teacher education, liberal education, and the liberal arts. Beginning with the relationship between liberal education and the liberal arts, those who cite the need for stronger liberal arts components in teacher education programs do so for two principal reasons. The first is that teachers need to be broadly educated, possessing at least some acquaintance with key ideas and works in social and cultural analysis and with the nature of the scientific enterprise.

This is not a contested position, any more than is the need for sound communication and quantitative skills, and the same imperatives hold for all students, including liberal arts majors. General education is an institutional goal, and it is the responsibility of college and university faculty to render their best judgment about what is most important in general education for all students and how that should be expressed in curricular terms. As I have noted already, periodic debate and revision of that judgment is not only inevitable, but should be seen as a healthful, vital part of faculty development and institutional identity. The resulting general education program may indeed be based on liberal arts courses, and there is always the hope that the program will be more imaginative and effective than a package of introductory disciplinary courses derived from interdepartmental log-rolling.

The second strand of reasoning behind advocating more liberal arts for teacher education, and the one on which I will concentrate, is seemingly more sophisticated. This is the claim by those in the liberal arts that the subject matter contained in liberal arts disciplines involves knowledge structures whose character is of a significantly different and superior order from those contained in teacher education curricula. These assertions of intellectual hierarchy, based on the nature of the subject matter, often include attempts to demonstrate that the differences between the types of knowledge in professional and liberal arts curricula correspond to the differences between, say, objective versus speculative and value-laden knowledge, or narrowness versus breadth, or a range of variations of Weber's instrumental knowledge versus substantive knowledge (e.g., Pickle, 1984; Rehnke, 1982–1983; Rice, 1983). These arguments are epistemologically dubious and encourage suspect claims about some knowledge being "intrinsically worth knowing." When they are not emphatically and cogently refuted, it is extremely easy and seemingly natural to define liberal education simply as education in liberal arts disciplines, a misleading conflation of ideas.

The identification of liberal education with the liberal arts means that the distinction between liberal education and teacher education (and other professional programs) is based primarily on conventions about *subject matter*. But these conventions merely reflect the various historical routes by which different subject matter entered U.S. colleges and universities, as well as an atavistic form of elitism. The definitions of what actually does comprise the subject matter of liberal arts disciplines are vague, incoherent, and susceptible to rapid, opportunistic changes. A convincing intellectual and pedagogical distinction between liberal arts disciplines and education as an academic field is, at the very least, elusive (Pietig, 1984; Webb & Sherman, 1983).

TEACHER EDUCATION AND LIBERAL EDUCATION

In spite of the dubious intellectual properties of academic disciplines, the liberal arts ideology exercises decisive hegemony in colleges and universities. Faculty in liberal arts disciplines have been quite successful in getting others to accept that they are the locus of superior forms of knowledge, the rightful proprietors of liberal education, and the genuine intellectual core of higher education.

The unavoidable corollary of these knowledge claims is that teacher education programs, *because of the putatively intrinsic properties of their subject matter*, are necessarily inferior to the real business of the institution and are to be tolerated only as long as student demand and external agencies make retaining these programs politically and fiscally expedient for the health of the institution as a whole. In this reading of the true and the right, the marginalization of education faculty and their programs within institutions of higher education takes on the appearance of being natural, proper, and easy.

It is imperative that, in defending themselves against charges of poor quality, education faculty avoid even appearing to accept terms that necessarily imply their own subordinate position within an intellectual hierarchy whose sources purportedly reside in the inherent nature of knowledge structures. That is, teacher educators need to be free from the myth that the administrative forms prevalent in higher education have genuine substantive and educational rationales. Instead of acquiescing to spurious knowledge claims about various subject matters, it is more in line with the historical tradition of liberal education, and also makes more educational and tactical sense, to argue that the *approaches* to knowledge involved in various courses and programs of study should be the primary criteria for distinguishing between significantly different types of educational endeavors.

This was argued at the end of Chapter 3, where training was contrasted with liberal education. *Training* was defined as the type of learning in which a body of information and techniques is considered to be inert and external to the student and teacher, and in which the teacher's role is to transmit this body of knowledge to students and to judge students' abilities to reproduce and apply it following prescribed procedures. On the other hand, *liberal education* was defined as the type of educational endeavor in which knowledge is seen to be multifaceted and to require interpretation. The role of the teacher, therefore, is to help students learn to use logic, evidence, and a sense of intellectual context to identify the role of premises, selection, and perspectives in others' analyses and, further, to construct and defend interpretations of their own, that is, engage self-consciously and critically in the creation of knowledge and the constitution of meaning.

When looked at in this way, it is clear that any subject in the liberal arts is fully capable of being taught as training. More to the point here, it is equally clear that the liberal arts do not hold a monopoly of subject matter appropriate for liberal education. Independent of possible quality problems among teacher education programs, the subject matter of education—say, elementary education—is important, requires close attention to context, and, in its complexity, calls for treatment from a variety of angles and at different levels of abstraction. The programs' subject matter, therefore, is fully capable of being organized and taught in ways that promote the development of students' critical intellects.[1]

After all, questions concerned with the human capacity to learn (including which people learn what) have been and should continue to be seen as central to a very large part of the Western intellectual tradition. The import and significance of these questions are enhanced when we address learning by young people, because in doing so we engage all of the rich issues about child development. These include the debate over how recently the idea of "childhood" as a distinct phase of life became dominant in Western culture (Aries, 1962); over nature versus nurture, and the implications for a democratic political order; over the meaning of youth cultures; over the rapidly changing racial and ethnic composition of school-age children; and so on.

Moreover, the study of teaching and learning should be set in appropriately specific contexts, and there is no doubt that schools are key social and cultural institutions, reflecting and influencing the directions of American thought and life by serving as intersections of civil and political forces as well as of personal anxieties. It is hard to come up with a significant social, scientific, or cultural issue that does not bear directly on teaching and learning or on schools and schooling, or in which exploring educational questions does not contribute to a deeper understanding of the issue.

The practical orientation of teacher education certainly does not condemn it to intellectually flat conceptions of purpose. Student teachers do need to know how to prepare lesson plans and to appreciate that certain methods of teaching reading and computation are more useful than others. Nevertheless, every prescription about proper lesson-plan development and every experiment designed to test the efficacy of a particular teaching method embodies myriad assumptions about the characteristics of the subject matter or skill being taught; the nature of human cognition; the backgrounds of students; the patterns of authority in the classroom, school, and system; and the relationship between schooling and society. It is by introducing these levels of analysis that the field of education becomes an intellectually compelling field of inquiry and that training courses become true liberal education courses. This is such compelling work that it is difficult to imagine how education as a field of study could ever be considered to be narrow or dull.

Furthermore, internships and the practicum offer invaluable opportunities for students to test conflicting approaches about teaching and learning in concrete settings, giving "academic" disputes a genuine immediacy that liberal arts disciplines in colleges across the nation are striving to emulate by developing "real-life," off-campus opportunities. There is nothing in state certification requirements, which necessarily are couched in general terms, to prevent education programs from being exciting, rigorous, and coherent learning experiences. State certification requirements, in and of themselves, provide excellent materials for educationally fruitful inquiry by students, as does the teaching profession, especially since its history is that of a women's profession.

This approach, emphasizing these levels of analysis and inquiry, is a vitally important pedagogical element for teacher training. From my own observation, it is precisely the compelling ·connections between practical skills and broader issues that kindles the intellectual excitement and enthusiasm for learning that characterize outstanding teachers. The appreciation of this approach is necessary for students to practice a similar pedagogy in their own teaching.

Finally, education as a subject matter has a coherence greater than most liberal arts disciplines. Even though one occasionally hears as a criticism or, depending on the source of the observation, a lament that there is no common "methodology" in education, education programs' theoretical eclecticism is not any greater than that of, say, sociology, history, anthropology, literature, philosophy, and political science. Further, the programs' clear focus on a specific subject matter enables disputes about key questions, interpretations, and approaches to be argued out on a more common basis than is available to any of the aforementioned disciplines.

Through the critical-inquiry approach to undergraduate education, then, it is clear that schools, schooling, teaching, and learning comprise an identifiable subject matter that is intrinsically important yet rarely included in liberal arts curricula. It is a subject area in which students' questions about the process of education can lead them to explore history, politics, science, language, and other fields in an integrated and meaningful manner. In addition, the complexity of the subject matter of teacher education requires close attention to contexts and enables treatment from a variety of angles and at various levels of abstraction. In other words, the subject matter, properly approached, can be the basis of an exciting and rigorous liberal education.

EXAMPLE OF A TEACHER EDUCATION PROGRAM

For the sake of an example, it would be feasible to organize an undergraduate education studies program for future teachers along lines different from the conventional and dubious theoretical/philosophical-versus-applied paradigm. An education studies program could be organized into two tracks, one focused on child development, cognition, and the classroom; the other on schools and schooling as social and cultural institutions. Both tracks would employ a critical-inquiry pedagogy and contain substantial multicultural content as routine course materials, and each student in teacher education, after completing the usual breadth requirements and demonstrating good abilities in writing, tabulating, information retrieval, and other skills, would choose to emphasize one of the two tracks in his or her studies.

Students working in either track who plan to become teachers at the secondary level would design and complete a concentration incorporating substantial academic work in both their chosen subject area for teaching, probably drawn mostly from liberal arts departments, and in education studies.

The first track, focusing on child development, cognition, and the classroom, would be strongly influenced by cognitive science, which, with its emphasis on theoretical and practical studies of human cognition, offers an intellectually more demanding and rewarding approach than standard educational psychology, with its behavioristic roots. Students who work in this track would choose or formulate concentrations around such issues as language acquisition, educational testing, environmental education, gender roles, and the place of mathematical and scientific learning in cognitive development.

The second track in education studies would focus on current educational issues in the United States, in their historical contexts. Student concentrations in this curriculum would be organized around such topics as teaching as a profession (including certification processes, unionization, and the historical role of women teachers), the changing character of schools' missions and purposes, public policy regarding education, economics of education, debates on social mobility and the screening function of education (with particular attention to racial minorities), the relation between educational ideology and politics, and the role of parents in educating their children.

The two education studies tracks could draw from courses throughout the institution and would be distinguished from each other primarily by their different focus and level of inquiry, and yet they would be closely related as well. Broadly conceived studies of educational institutions must be informed by a solid understanding of child development and learning theory; conversely, studies of teaching and learning must be firmly set in more general historical and social contexts, to give meaning to studies at the level of the classroom. An introductory core course for each curriculum would be required for all education studies students, and each would stress the strong relationships between the two levels of study.

If the introductory core courses were structured in ways consistent with the principles outlined here, they would also be attractive to other students. In fact, an important goal of the education studies program would be to serve, at all levels of study, a wide variety of liberal arts and other professional students who were interested in children, public policy, cognition, social institutions, or other issues that would be integral parts of the education studies program. In this program, teacher certification would be an option for those who wished to become teachers, but the program would be a solid and exciting liberal education program similar to all others in that it would be suitable for students with a wide variety of occupational interests. This mix of students would itself enrich the education studies programs, which too often are now populated by only prospective teachers.

Although I am not familiar with the teacher certification requirements of all 50 states, judging from the increasingly flexible requirements of the New England states, it would not be too difficult, even if it required a bit of creativity in choosing course titles, to fashion an interesting and intellectually challenging teacher education that both satisfied state requirements and did not allow those requirements to dictate either the structure or content of the program.

Certification would necessitate special advising, as it always does, and some concentrations lend themselves more readily to having certification requirements integrated into coherent and substantive study programs than others. If a student did elect to become certified (especially for elementary school teaching), this would to a certain extent guide a student's choice of concentration, but it definitely would not determine that the student must (or be able to) forego a liberal education.

The education studies program proposed here is significantly different from those at many liberal arts colleges with teacher education programs. The field of education is not added onto liberal education programs, or onto liberal arts programs, but rather is a self-conscious liberal education program that has the potential of assuming leadership in institutional debates about liberal education.

CONCLUDING REMARKS

Schools, schooling, teaching, and learning comprise an identifiable and coherent subject matter that is intrinsically important, lends itself readily to excellent liberal education programs, and is disgracefully ignored by liberal arts curricula. The conclusion from this argument is inevitably double edged. Teacher education programs should not tolerate being relegated to second-class academic citizenship because of specious claims about different properties of knowledge. On the other hand, these programs cannot use the nature of their subject matter as an excuse for offering curricula that are anything other than demanding, rigorous, and exciting. While it is routine for leading teacher educators to call for closer relations with the teaching profession, it probably is at least as important right now for them to become more fully integrated into the colleges and universities in which teacher education programs are located. They must demand and deserve respect as full-fledged academics, a process that will entail teacher education programs' becoming sources of intellectual vitality and of general pedagogical insight and initiation within the institutions.

7

Black Studies, White Studies: Goals and Strategies

Throughout the 1960s and 1970s, the numbers of black Americans (or African-Americans) attending colleges and universities rose substantially in absolute numbers and in proportion to total enrollments. Even though black Americans were disproportionately enrolled in community colleges, there were significant gains in attendance at four-year institutions and in graduate programs. During the same period, however, the representation of blacks in many graduate professional schools declined (S. T. Hill, 1981, 1983; Morris, 1981), and, beginning in the middle of the 1970s, their proportional representation in all graduate and undergraduate programs began to decline.

In absolute numbers, undergraduate enrollments by African-American students peaked in 1979–1980 and have generally declined through the 1980s. Meanwhile, the numbers and proportional representation of black high school graduates were rising to new heights (Carnegie Foundation, 1987b; "1986 Minority Enrollment," 1988). The tone set by elected and appointed federal officials, changes in federal student aid and loan policies, a new and less comfortable climate on campus for black students, disadvantageous changes in earning patterns by black workers, increased attractiveness of the armed services for careers and vocational training, and other factors have played into these new trends (Arbeiter, 1987).

It is extremely important, therefore, that a college and university education become more attractive and feasible for African-Americans. Black studies programs have a crucial role to play in this effort; however, at predominantly white colleges and universities, such programs are badly pressed, because, like black students, they have never been especially welcome in the white academy. Debates about the advisability and usefulness of such programs have raged for years, and with the financial reversals in higher education, the stakes have risen.

THE CASE FOR BLACK STUDIES

Academic rationales for black studies usually emphasize the intrinsic importance and integrity of the subject matter, long ignored and devalued in traditional curricula and scholarship. This line of argument put forward by its advocates often includes the contention that black studies is a genuine academic discipline in its own right. There are two other prominent components of the case for black studies. One is that a formal black studies program is crucial for providing institutional resources for black students trying to survive in an alien (and frequently hostile) environment. The other is that such a program is a means by which institutions can meet their obligation to make a clear, public statement about race and racism through the most potent media available to them—their curricula and catalogues.

All of these dimensions are vitally important for black studies programs, but, in advocating them, the various dimensions must be linked together in a plausible and productive way. When they stand alone, each one has some serious political pitfalls. Before suggesting what I believe is a promising framework for combining these dimensions into a unified, cogent argument, it is worth mentioning some of the problems likely to be encountered when the elements are used in isolation.

White Guilt

Pressuring institutions to make a statement is often a subtle or not-so-subtle use of white guilt. While this may result in an institution's public commitment to black studies, there is a large and depressing volume of evidence that white guilt is a weak and not dependable reed, capable of turning into its opposite in the form of quite nasty backlashes. Even without the backlash, white guilt is capable of leading the institution to promote a variety of institutional policies and patronizing attitudes not necessarily desirable from the standpoint of black studies and black students.

Supportive Academic Environment

There is no question about the importance of appropriately tailored arrangements and support for African-American students, but too much emphasis on these students' special needs can easily make the whole endeavor vulnerable to charges that black studies is merely a special-interest cover for academically weak students.

This should be avoided, and there are two points about academic standards in respect to black students that should be kept in mind. First, discussions about academic standards in general are usually characterized by outstandingly complacent and flaccid rhetoric. There is a persistent tendency for the faculty to employ phrases like "students not measuring up to standards." This is a pernicious avoidance of teachers' major responsibilities, which are more accurately represented in the phrase, "bringing students up to standards." The two phrases might sound somewhat alike, but their connotations embody a profound difference in attitude. It is the difference between screening and educating, a distinction that is not, of course, racially neutral.

The second point about academic standards is in regard to the continuing dispute over whether or not the poor scores recorded by black Americans on the Scholastic Aptitude Test (SAT) are due to a severe and consistent cultural bias in the structure of the test. The purpose of the SAT is to predict the probability of an applicant's succeeding academically in a college or university. There is some evidence that SAT scores by black Americans do indeed underpredict subsequent academic performance, but on this level it seems clear that a mechanically applied technical adjustment can easily be made to remedy the problem. While it may be difficult to deal with the cautious and scientistic SAT bureaucracy, the necessary adjustments could easily be made by individual admissions officers. If the admissions officers are unwilling, however, to multiply black applicants' SAT scores by whatever factor it has been determined will make them more genuinely comparable to the scores of other applicants, they are likely to find other reasons to deny admissions to black candidates. The recent experience of Asian candidates with very high SAT scores illustrates this potential.

It seems to me, however, that the specific properties of the test bear only marginally on the issue at hand. Again, the purpose of the SAT is to predict college and university applicants' academic success in higher education institutions, and black test takers do not fare as well on the test as whites. There are two approaches to this issue that appear to be more productive than criticizing the test.

The first is that the results of the SAT may indeed be an accurate measure of the result of the society's unwillingness to educate black students as well as white students. There are many sources of direct, independent corroboration of this uneven allocation of educational resources and opportunities, and it is not surprising to find that, as a consequence, black students do not score as well on the test. Do those who focus on the unfairness of the SAT scores believe that black Americans are educated as well as whites in our society? If blacks and whites were to score similarly well, the test would certainly be suspect. As it is, however, the differential test scores stand both as a continuing indictment of educational policy in respect to those already disadvantaged in multiple ways, as well as a potent weapon to rectify those policies. Apart from genetic fetishism, SAT scores are politically useful ammunition in the real fight.

The second approach is to remember that SAT scores predict success in college and university work, and of course these are, by and large, white colleges and universities. Whatever important cultural bias exists is manifest in this side of things as well as in the test, which supposedly is trying to gauge students' likely success in academies designed and organized by whites for whites. (I discuss the significance of white studies later in this chapter.)

Black Studies As a Discipline

Arguing that black studies is an authentic academic discipline employs the very same terms of reference—complete with underlying premises—used by that garden-variety opponent who argues that black studies subject matter and black students could be taught better under the auspices of established disciplinary departments. Disciplinary departments, so the story goes, represent coherent and well-defined categories of knowledge and thus are the best guarantors of intellectual rigor and standards. A close scrutiny of the character of academic disciplines reveals the inaccuracy of this view. As discussed in Chapter 1, the peculiar nature of academic disciplines is much better understood by regarding them as principally self-serving professional bodies whose existence is based primarily on the coordinated exercise of power over certification and academic legitimacy.

The abysmal record of the social sciences and humanities in respect to their treatment of black issues and black academics amply testifies to the properties of the disciplines. Issues of race were considered worthy of teaching by these disciplines when and only when social control mechanisms broke down in the 1960s, and the particular form of blacks' oppression became a problem for white society. Even then, student pressure and federal research largess were necessary inducements for some aspects of the black experience to be included in these disciplines. Now that the heat is off and federal funding for research on black issues has virtually dried up, racially specific questions, content, and angles of vision are rapidly being moved even further to the peripheries of disciplines.

What this all means, then, is that academic disciplines simply are not based on inherent and universal intellectual qualities; the burden of proof in regard to teaching effectiveness and standards, therefore, needs to weigh as heavily on the more traditional disciplinary departments as on black studies units. Of course, without some extraordinary occurrence, that burden of proof will belong to black studies and to other new units (e.g., women's studies, Chicano studies, and so on). Thus we are taken right back to the arena of institutional politics and unequal power.

In attempting to work for some advantage in this arena, invoking the disciplinary mystique may be good tactics in certain circumstances, but one must be very careful about commiting black studies programs to these terms. The definition of disciplines is infinitely elastic, and those solidly entrenched in disciplinary departments can easily shift the defining characteristics of disciplines among subject matter, methodology, and level of analysis, to the disadvantage of black studies. It may be politically productive, and even amusing, to expose this academic shell game, but it is dangerous to attach the case for black studies too firmly to the illusions of disciplinary professionalism.

A STRATEGY FOR MAKING THE CASE

The principal purpose of this chapter is to propose an approach that welds together the major goals of black studies (including some administrative autonomy) into a unified conception capable of preserving and developing the value of the subject matter and at the same time of couching the argument in language that is politically palatable to the faculty and administrators of predominantly white colleges and universities. The best way to begin is with a very academic type of rationale and to pitch it at a level in which institutions have the least confidence: their general missions and purposes.

Colleges and universities—and especially their undergraduate liberal arts divisions—seldom articulate their purposes with any precision, and this confusion is clearly expressed by the grandiosity and vacuous generalities of their catalogue mission statements (Baldridge et al., 1978; Bowen, 1980). In spite of their chronic penchant for the banal and gratuitous, mission statements can be useful, for almost invariably somewhere in the list of academic goals there are references to developing students' capacities for independent and critical thinking, intellectual flexibility, learning how to learn, and other similar intellectual competencies.

Here is the opportunity: Black studies advocates ought to move to strengthen those sections of the mission statement that define the educational enterprise as one that promotes qualities of mind and habits of rigorous thinking by students, and to do so at the expense of sections that imply that education is principally a matter of transferring information. This can be done by appealing to the need to strengthen the "distinguished tradition of liberal learning" at the institution, and so forth, but the real case will no doubt rest on other grounds.

Liberal arts faculty need to be convinced—with some subtlety, of course—that, when students' assimilation of "neutral information" and "value-free techniques" is truly considered to be the essence of education, their status and even livelihoods are seriously jeopardized. The acceptance of an institutional mission predicated wholly or even in good part on "education as transmission" should immediately raise the specter of administrators' replacing faculty with technologically sophisticated electronic processors that really are efficient, do not talk back to deans, keep office hours, and never ask for raises.

Faculty have been rather slow in catching on to the fact that definitions of education based on notions of coverage and transmission are extremely dangerous to them in very tangible ways. Their self-interest is best served by vigorously pushing the principles that no information is neutral (i.e., independent of interpretation), that techniques embody important assumptions about the world that indelibly influence results, that education should enable students to live and work with this situation in responsible and effective ways, and that live teachers are necessary to teach the complexities of multidimensional knowledge. Even though in practice they may simply be pouring information and techniques into students' ears, most faculty do like to believe that they are teaching students how to think.

The point of all this is that, once the principle is accepted, even if only in a general and unarticulated way, there are strong corollaries that follow. One such corollary is especially beneficial to the case for a black studies program, and that is that a good education requires alternative perspectives on knowledge. Diverse interpretations should be nurtured and institutionalized, because diversity is both integral and necessary for the quality of the educational experience, and not just a luxury to be tolerated—much less persecuted. In this milieu, the role of a formal black studies program is rather compelling.

The idea that black studies offers a different and useful perspective on knowledge is certainly neither new nor profound. Still, when identified with the educational mission of the college and current fearfulness on the part of the faculty, it can become very useful in political maneuvering. Another advantage to this particular approach is that it can be based on the idea that the new and desirable angle of vision is due to the *content* of black studies (Davidson, Dodson, & Ross, 1982). The argument that it is the content of the program that offers the additional perspective avoids the trap of a "coverage" rationale, and it also means that black studies will not be expected to present some unified, homogeneous, and invariably sanitized "black perspective," as the discipline route might seem to prescribe. The value of this feature is that there is no need to curtail productive methodological and theoretical debates among black studies faculty in order to maintain some artificial unity, which, of course, none of the other academic programs can, or should, sustain.

In another extremely important facet of institutional politics, this strategy is much more likely to achieve strong alliances with partisans of (white) women's studies, Hispanic studies, Native American studies, and various types of international and comparative programs, than is the disciplinary argument, which necessarily casts the other programs in the role of competitors with black studies. Since the type of competition fostered by the disciplinary approach accepts the institution's current educational concepts, even if one or more of these aspiring programs does gain formal recognition, the victories do little to expand the prevailing idea of higher education in generally progressive ways and may impede similar recognition of others.

BLACK STUDIES AND WHITE STUDIES

The emphasis here has indeed been on seeking out advantageous grounds for campus infighting, but the value of the approach suggested here is not limited to political expediency. The purposes of black studies programs have not been compromised; rather, they have been made capable of a systematic and interesting formulation that should be helpful to the people directly involved.

This is especially evident in respect to the major functions of black studies—the education of students, black and white. That is, the articulation of a clear stance toward knowledge by black studies faculty members should encourage students to understand that what is being taught throughout the institution—including its very categories of knowledge—has been developed by particular people in specific historical circumstances. Put plainly, it is whites who have selected facts and formulated questions and methods in ways consistent with the interests, values, and aspirations of white society. For better or worse, white studies is overwhelmingly what a college education has to offer in the way of learning.

The manner in which individual black studies programs set out to teach this perspective will vary. One axis along which different programs will be differentially located is in the relative mix between conveying this understanding directly through courses explicitly oriented to epistemology and the sociology of knowledge, and indirectly through courses on the black experience itself.

As has been implied, the emphasis on perspective does not mean that all white studies subject matter is so thoroughly racist that it is dangerous to or useless for nonwhite peoples. In fact, it is vital for black students to master white studies, so they will have the skills, information, and insight into patterns of thought necessary (although clearly not sufficient) for freeing themselves from white domination. This has its obvious dangers, but a sustained emphasis on different perspectives on knowledge can enable black students to acquire in white studies, the tools for understanding the destructive and contradictory character of the ideology by which they are oppressed. Without consistently stressing the interpretive character of knowledge, it is considerably more difficult for black students to learn white studies without accepting white studies' own view of itself as the universal alternative to ignorance—an acceptance that entails a corrosive denial of both self and heritage.

The argument, then, is that the development of a coherent and persuasive general approach to higher education oriented toward the development of students' independent and critical thinking is both instrumentally and intrinsically valuable for black studies advocates. This strategy would allow black studies proposals to identify with traditions of higher education that, although seldom practiced, still exercise considerable ideological hegemony in academia, turn current faculty anxieties in a productive direction, reduce damaging competition with other potentially progressive segments of the academy, and encourage productive theoretical and methodological debates within black studies.

Moreover, stressing multiple perspectives on knowledge is worthwhile in its own right. By this approach, black studies programs can help African-American students to see that competence in white studies is desirable, while maintaining a sense of proportion about its place in the scheme of things. This point of view is important for all students but imperative for black students, who can be shown that they can succeed in white studies without becoming white, and that it really does matter.

8

Introductory Statistics
and Liberal Education

This chapter argues two closely related propositions. First, some knowledge of statistics should be considered to be an important element of undergraduate education. Second, moving students too quickly into advanced levels of quantitative analysis, at the expense of a thorough grounding in the uses of descriptive statistics (e.g., tabular and graphical presentations, properties of averages and other summary statistics, and so on), seriously impedes the liberal education potential of introductory statistics courses, especially in the social sciences. The first section of this chapter makes a case for the greater recognition of statistics as an element of liberal education, while the second illustrates the way in which an introductory statistics course can be appropriate for liberal education purposes.

LIBERAL EDUCATION AND NUMBERS

Mathematical study was prominent in the medieval quadrivium, and the value of mathematics for undergraduate education continues to be acknowledged, even if in a very general manner. Systematic use of quantitative evidence, however, is considerably more recent than the quadrivium. Perhaps because those outside the statistics discipline tend to view the study of statistics in narrowly instrumental terms (i.e., of acquiring a kit of tools in preparation for more advanced work in their disciplines), there has been too little consideration of the broader importance of statistics in undergraduate education.[1]

Including statistics as a component of undergraduate education is certainly consistent with the principles of eighteenth- and nineteenth-century educational theory. For example, the computations involved in constructing a series of tables can be seen as valuable for training the faculties of memory and attention, and the understanding and application of computational rules are good exercise for developing the faculty of reasoning. Furthermore, anyone who has spent the long hours required to generate or to locate and recompute the quantitative evidence appropriate for a specific proposition and then to figure out how to present it in a clear and cogent manner will appreciate that the process certainly could be considered to promote discipline, will, and character, other important educational goals during the last century (Kolesnik, 1958).

The broader educational value of studying statistics, however, does not rest on the shaky tenets of eigteenth-century psychology. The second step of my argument is that a carefully constructed introductory statistics course in which students confront questions about whether specific data are or are not consistent with particular claims, even without exploring fundamental epistemological questions, can promote educationally productive habits of mind and attitudes toward learning. For instance, quantitative materials are especially useful for demonstrating, in a tangible and readily comprehensible fashion, the differences among various kinds of knowing and the imperative of clearly distinguishing among different levels of analysis (or abstraction).

Moreover, as an integral part of the effort to encourage habits of systematic, critical thinking, the subject matter of statistics readily lends itself to pedagogical formats conducive to convincing students that learning requires continuous and active involvement by them as well as by the teacher. This last assertion might seem rather odd for an area of study whose goals too often appear to be no more than the mechanical transmission of a fixed set of skills to students.

While the cookbook statistics course is a familiar caricature, there is no more need for the statistics teacher's function to be reduced to pouring inert knowledge into passive students than there is for teachers in any other field. Quantitative data most certainly do not speak for themselves, and the same body of data can be (and often is) used to support divergent conclusions. Moreover, the selection of what is counted, as well as the very categories in which data are collected and presented, necessarily entails making premises, limiting the types of questions that can be addressed to the data, and influencing the range of answers deemed plausible. This clearly is a very important area for promoting educational goals of the critical inquiry kind.

An appreciation for the interpretive latitude permitted (and required) by quantitative materials, even when the boundaries of that latitude are continually stressed, enables an introductory statistics course to avoid being dominated by complex techniques of statistical inference and thereby to emphasize introducing students to the means and necessity of creating their own interpretations of quantitative evidence and of intelligently criticizing others' uses of it. Among the central aims of such a course, then, is to convince students that learning to deal effectively with quantitative materials is important, that it requires the students' active engagement, and that the necessary engagement is feasible and even rewarding. Systematic thinking and creative conceptions of knowledge and learning are integral to the aims of liberal education and are crucial for an extremely wide range of advanced study, whether that study involves analyzing literary texts, interpreting historical processes, or assessing the significance of laboratory findings.

Finally, the third step in my argument is that, even if one were to reject all conceptions of education embodying notions of mental discipline and the "transfer of training," thereby defining the goals of undergraduate education strictly in terms of covering essential areas of knowledge and imparting key skills, statistics still should be regarded as a valuable element in that education. Statistics is an extremely important area of knowledge in its own right. While private financial record keeping has a very long history, the quantitative study of social questions began only in seventeenth-century England. Although German influences were significant during the eighteenth century, the extensive development of national social statistics is primarily a legacy of the nineteenth-century English "statistics movement," which in large part was the product of the Victorians' concern with social reform and control (Cullen, 1975).

Social reform impulses continue to wax and wane, but the propensity to count everything "important" not only remains, but has flourished impressively. As a consequence, we are now at a point where so much of our understanding of contemporary social existence is constructed and communicated through the use of statistics that quantitative literacy is critical for effective participation in social and political life. In our culture, the ability to find and interpret quantitative material is a prerequisite for gaining access to important types of social knowledge, for formulating plausible arguments, and for distinguishing between legitimate and illegitimate use of the statistics with which we are deluged in everyday life. It is silly and irresponsible to dismiss or to accept uncritically arguments based on statistics; neutrality is not a tenable position.

Although by no means mutually exclusive, these three layers of argument are based on different conceptions of learning and the purposes of education, and together they form a strong case for the vital importance of including some knowledge of statistics in the definition of liberal education. The third element of my argument is predicated primarily on dealing with social statistics, which foreshadows the next section and its discussion of introductory statistics courses in the social sciences.

DESCRIPTIVE STATISTICS AND PEDAGOGY

Economics and psychology are the most quantitative of the social science disciplines; sociology is not far behind; quantitative history, especially in the "new social history," is perhaps the fastest growing area of the discipline; political science is rather uneven in regard to the use of quantitative methods; and even in anthropology there is increasing interest in the applications of quantitative techniques. An introductory statistics course is a common requirement for undergraduate economics, psychology, and sociology majors, and, even when it is not required, it is frequently recommended strongly. These introductory statistics courses, however, are too often viewed as merely necessary nuisances by students and faculty. While the quantitative skills represented in them are valued for advanced work in the discipline, the benefits of those skills are realized only elsewhere, and the courses are too often taken and taught with considerable reluctance by all participants.

As I asserted earlier, a strong emphasis on descriptive statistics is the best way for an introductory course to achieve broader educational aims for students. While this remains my principal point, there also are strong pedagogical reasons for emphasizing descriptive statistics, even in courses that eschew these larger aims and aspire only to the more limited goals for disciplinary majors. In order to address both the liberal education and the skills acquisition aspects in a suitably concrete manner, I will focus on the teaching of statistics in one social science—economics. I have chosen economics because it is the discipline I know best, and because the tendencies I have observed in the teaching materials for introductory economics statistics are discernible in other social sciences.[2] Therefore, while the particular examples may be relevant only for economists, the general issues should be of interest and concern to a wider range of teachers.

In the introductory statistics course for economics majors, the primary aims should be a solid introduction to handling and reasoning from descriptive statistics (including the significance of the categories in which data are collected and presented), the advantages of different ways in which such statistics can be presented for particular purposes, and the important corpus of systematically collected and published economic data. Instead of starting a course with throwing dice and flipping coins, my experience suggests that there is no substitute for devoting the first few weeks to having students experiment with different tabular and graphical arrangements of data, in order to increase their ability to use tables and graphs effectively and to appreciate problems of construction and interpretation. Through this experience, students should become familiar with at least the following: how the purpose of displaying data governs the selection of empirical information; the need to be careful with units of measure and their time dimensions (e.g., stocks versus flows); the proper use of averages, measures of dispersion, percentages, index numbers, and so on; and, not quite parallel, the use of a calculator and perhaps a computer terminal.

These exercises need not be as deadening as they sound. One effective device is to distribute several pages of actual figures on, for instance, wages and salaries for a number of years, cross-classified by industrial and occupational groupings and by race, age, gender, region, and so on. Right away, the teacher can demonstrate, in specific and interesting ways, a variety of techniques for displaying data to illuminate various changes over time, while at the same time introducing the classification schemes by which industrial, occupational, and other data are arranged.

After students have been initiated in this manner, price indexes can be introduced to deflate nominal figures. The choice of which price indexes are appropriate for this purpose necessarily involves a discussion of coverage, the relative weights given to individual prices, basing periods in which comparisons are made, and other construction problems with a direct carry-over to quantity indexes. From here it is an easy step to circulate data on the distribution of income among families and individuals and to construct a host of statistical indicators on this dimension, including graphical devices.

There are many questions to be addressed. For example, in defining family income, why use the category of Personal Income rather than that of Disposable Income? Why have these aggregates constituted changing proportions of the Gross National Product and the National Income over time? Such concepts and alternatives should be briefly explained. After treating national income aggregates, it is easy and natural to explore national income accounts.

By this time, students should be able to look at a wide variety of data presentations and be able to discern what they are about. Thus they will be ready for input/output tables and flow-of-funds accounts, and, with some additional discussion of sampling techniques, they should deal very easily with such survey data as unemployment figures, industrial concentration ratios, and leading indicators of economic activity.

Throughout the course, it is essential that these explorations be guided by provocative, nontrivial questions on which the data can shed some light. Do the data show that men earn more than women? How does race affect this? By using a simple device like shift-share analysis, we can try to determine whether these differences in income move or do not move in concert with other variables, such as age and educational background.

The use of such questions not only helps sustain student interest in the whole endeavor, but provides a means by which students themselves can make arguments and interpretations from the data and get acquainted with several different sources. Useful references for these purposes include the *Statistical Abstract of the United States*, the *Historical Statistics* volumes, the *Economic Report of the President*, the *Survey of Current Business*, the *Federal Reserve Bulletin*, the *Monthly Labor Review*, and perhaps some census data, including industrial censuses and other surveys by the Department of Commerce.[3]

At any one of several points in the course, students can be exposed to the ideas of probable association between variables (e.g., through Philips curves or cross-sectional versus time series consumption functions), correlation and causation, frequency distributions, and elementary economic modeling and estimation procedures. But the major point here is that this should be done only after students have acquired a sound understanding of descriptive statistics that makes these topics less abstract, serves as an excellent background for an advanced course in econometrics and forecasting, and is immediately applicable in such other aspects of college life as writing term papers or reading newspapers.

CONCLUDING REMARKS

The purpose of this chapter goes beyond proposing a specific structure for a course. The preceding discussion, illustrating the feasibility of incorporating descriptive statistics into the center of an introductory course for economics majors, suggests the value of such a course design even in the narrower, tool-of-study conception of statistics instruction. Liberal education and the initial stages of specialized education can coincide, and the same resources of faculty and curriculum can serve both purposes extremely well.

By treating descriptive statistics in more than a casual and abbreviated manner in the introductory or general course, teachers provide a vital pedagogical step for students' comprehension of the more sophisticated quantitative methods essential for advanced study in social science disciplines. In economics, confidence in handling descriptive statistics is necessary for students to attach meaning to even such elementary calculations as single-equation least squares and correlation coefficients. Without sufficient care in the more pedestrian realm of data organization and presentation, the idea of fitting a line to a series of data points is extremely abstract for many students; in defense, they learn by rote and avoid more active engagement with quantitative work.

Within the specialized goals of the major curricula for the social sciences, the introductory statistics course ought to be the place where students learn the vitally important quantitative measures, the empirical magnitudes of social processes, the ways to find reliable data on their own, and the first-order issues involved in applying theoretical frameworks to data. Such a course, the effectiveness of which is greatly enhanced by being organized around a series of substantive questions, serves as an initiation into the knowledge of the discipline for those who will continue its study. Coordinated with other courses, an introductory statistics course should be regarded as one of the key components of liberal education as well as of the major curriculum.

It is always gratifying to find some underlying harmonies of interest, and the qualities that make descriptive statistics useful for furthering specialized disciplinary study are precisely those that also contribute to broader educational goals. In addition to confronting quantitative claims by advertisers and the overwhelming volume of economic data so assiduously reported in the mass media, people are continually required to assess important arguments purportedly based on quantitative facts about age, race, gender, family structure, marital status, religion, residential location, migration, health, crime, public sector budgets, educational attainment, intelligence, voting patterns, and on and on. In all of this, the confidence and the capacity to handle and interpret data *on the descriptive level* will significantly contribute to people's ability to function as informed citizens capable of independent judgments about what is "proven" by statistics.

We cannot let either our hostility to quantitative analysis or, at the other pole, our fascination with highly sophisticated statistical techniques and complex computational technologies obscure the very real value of designing statistics courses to achieve multiple goals and, in the process, making them better courses in respect to each set of goals.

9

Scholarship for Teaching Faculty

Good undergraduate education depends directly and immediately on the intellectual vitality of faculty. This statement is certainly a platitude and probably a tautology, but it is striking that, in the rapid growth of literature and programs directed at what is said to be faculty and instructional development, the intellectual component of faculty work is all but completely neglected.

CRITIQUE OF FACULTY DEVELOPMENT

In perusal of over two thousand pages of published analyses and case studies of instructional and faculty development, I discovered an almost exclusive concentration on pedagogical techniques and methods and on affective concerns by those prominent in the faculty development field. In spite of the emphasis on teaching in this literature, the virtual absence of citations to works in such journals as *College Teaching, Sociology of Education,* and *Biology Teacher* is remarkable. The vast majority of references employed by faculty development specialists are to each other.

By emphasizing teaching techniques, these academic development specialists implicitly assume that the content of college teaching is fixed and that issues about intellectual substance are of only secondary importance in improving teaching. This is precisely the premise commonly employed to denigrate teaching and to justify its low status in the academic profession. Knowledge, acuity, and imagination are not, of course, sufficient for good teaching, and there is no question about the value of, say, recent work on the stages of student cognitive development (especially Katz & Henry, 1988), the use of videotapes that enables us to see ourselves as others see us, and good suggestions about how to promote class discussions. But their value is derived wholly from a clear sense of the purposes of undergraduate education and from *what* is taught. Discussions of faculty development that ignore matters of educational purpose, content, and the stances toward that content are, therefore, seriously deficient. The techniques of survey research, social psychology, and group process and therapy, which appear to comprise the methodological bases of the new faculty development profession, are inadequate even to pose, much less debate, key educational questions that bear immediately and significantly on teaching quality.

For instance, these tendencies are clearly illustrated in the oft-cited book by Jerry Gaff (1975), a revealing example of the avoidance of content issues in faculty development circles. A table on page 6, under the heading "Faculty Development," lists "Intellectual base: clinical, developmental, and social psychology; psychiatry; socialization"; and under the heading "Instructional Development" lists "Intellectual base: education; instructional media and technology; learning theory; systems theory." How could such an obviously important area as content be so ignored?

In criticizing the technique orientation of current faculty development efforts, however, I am most emphatically not proposing a return to earlier notions that blithely assumed that increasing research opportunities would lead automatically to better teaching. There is widespread agreement on the inadequacy of this notion of faculty and instructional development, but current faculty development approaches seem to have reacted against this discredited notion in a way that leaves entirely intact its principal and most damaging tenet, namely, that there exists a qualitative distinction between the creation of knowledge and the transmission of knowledge.

To avoid this positivist trap, instructional development programs should stress the intellectual and scholarly character of faculty work, but they need to do so *in the context of the faculty's teaching.* This does not deny the importance of affective concerns or of research on teaching and pedagogical methods, but all of these need to be placed in a perspective based on an understanding of the implications of worthy educational goals and on the clear and operational acknowledgment that, first and foremost, teaching is an intellectual endeavor.[1]

A strong corollary of this position is that scholarship and publication are important components of continuing development of teaching faculty as intellectuals. While I emphatically agree that teaching should be the primary criterion for faculty recruitment, retention, and reward, faculty scholarship and *publication* (please note the emphasis) are extremely important in increasing teaching quality.[2]

CASE FOR FACULTY SCHOLARSHIP

Before directly arguing this proposition, it is worth noting that there are good reasons to encourage writing and publishing by teaching faculty, beyond their direct contributions to good teaching (and to our understanding of the world we inhabit). All faculty have received considerable investments of resources in their educations. These resources are ultimately social resources, and they continue to sustain faculty as intellectuals in a society that badly needs more in the way of informed, critical insights into the workings of natural, social, and cultural processes. I believe, therefore, that all faculty have an obligation to return some of the value of that social investment, in addition to teaching the students who attend a particular college or university. An important facet of this responsibility, and one that academic professionalization has discouraged, is to address publics outside of the academy. This case has been made by Jacoby (1987). Even if a faculty member's "broader audience" is limited to teachers at other institutions, however, there is quite a bit that needs to be said.

Continuing the discussion about the less obvious facets of the importance of faculty scholarship, a second reason for encouraging more writing and publishing among faculty is to increase the recognition of the faculty's institution as a place of intellectual vitality and ferment. The resulting heightened visibility and reputation is crucial in times of sharp competition among colleges and universities for students. The sad fact is that the time has passed when this type of concern could remain the exclusive province of nonacademic administrators. Moreover, this visibility increases the value of the letterhead and signature on letters of recommendation for students.

Finally, student evaluations of teaching are probably weakest in assessing the intellectual dimension of a faculty member's teaching effectiveness. Convincing documentation of intellectual vitality in the files of candidates for reappointment, tenure, and promotion is difficult to come by without having those candidates' tangible intellectual work reviewed by disinterested outsiders. Oral presentations are notoriously slippery bases for evaluation, and the use of outsiders to evaluate a faculty member's unpublished written work at the time of the review often runs the risk of less than candid responses. Just in the nature of the enterprise, it takes much less effort to write a blandly complimentary assessment than a trenchantly critical one. Evaluators also probably regard the personnel committee at a teaching-oriented college to be substantially less important than the editorial board of a professional journal. As a consequence, referees' assessments of manuscripts addressed to journal editors are likely to be more careful and painstaking than the ad hoc, relatively private assessments of a faculty member's unpublished scholarship addressed to college personnel committees, even when written by the same people.

Although these elements are worth keeping in mind, it is imperative that scholarship not be regarded exclusively in its punitive guise, a means for "raising standards" and threatening vulnerable, untenured faculty members (who not just incidentally are disproportionately female and minority). In contrast, my principal argument for encouraging, supporting, and rewarding scholarship by teaching faculty is to enhance teaching quality.

In many institutions that stress teaching quality, however, there is an active hostility toward faculty scholarship. This does not make sense for colleges that are not afraid of ideas and debate. But even in colleges where there is a clear antischolarship ideology, the issue of research and publication continues to live on as a source of tension among faculty, among departments, and between faculty and administrators.

But, as I have said, the principal case I wish to make is in regard to its contribution to good teaching. In the literature on higher education, concern about the quality of undergraduate teaching seems to have *increased* doubt about the place that writing for publication should occupy in the professional lives of undergraduate teaching faculty. For instance, while there are differences among three recent reports on higher education issued by the National Institute of Education (Study Group, 1984), the American Association of Colleges (Project on Redefining, 1985), and the Carnegie Foundation (Boyer, 1987), all have lent considerable prestige to the proposition that writing for publication does not contribute to (and may even detract from) quality teaching. This conclusion is based on the notion that the relationship between teaching and scholarship is limited to that of competition. It is an easy step, then, to go from this conviction about competitiveness to the conclusion that, since undergraduate faculty's overriding responsibility is to teach, they should not divert their energies into writing for publication (which for convenience I simply call "scholarship"). The reasoning behind this conclusion needs careful scrutiny, because some of the arguments are based on weak and misleading premises.

It is important to digress for a moment here to explain that, while my language may appear to exclude the visual and performing artists, the argument applies as much to them as to their bookish colleagues. My use of terms and examples, and the seeming exclusion, is due to expediency rather than conviction. For instance, the meaning of *scholarship* in this chapter should be understood to incorporate performances, showings, designs, compositions, and other public presentations by artists, in addition to the more conventionally understood research, writing, and publishing.

So, to reiterate, there is no question that teaching effectiveness should be the primary criterion for rewarding faculty in undergraduate institutions. Furthermore, at some level of involvement teaching and scholarship are definitely competitive. There are only 168 hours in a week. The appropriate conclusion to draw from these propositions, however, is that undergraduate institutions must make explicit provision for faculty to engage in scholarship, because there are substantial and often overlooked *complementarities* between good teaching and faculty scholarship. This notion is not widely understood. Even in the case of faculty engaged in liberal education, which I will emphasize, the three reports cited earlier assert that scholarly engagement and teaching quality are essentially independent activities, except in that they compete for faculty time and energy. This frequently heard assertion is based on two serious misconceptions. One involves the nature of undergraduate liberal education and teaching, and the second concerns the range of scholarship considered useful and serious. The result of these misconceptions is a distorted understanding about the relationship between teaching and scholarship.

Scholarship and the Character of Undergraduate Teaching

As already noted, techniques of presentation, pace of assignments, and methods for stimulating class discussion are important factors in teaching effectiveness, and it is this level that is emphasized heavily (if not exclusively) by teaching evaluation instruments. Without detracting from the necessity of good communication and classroom management skills, it is time to present a clear argument that excellent undergraduate teaching needs to be understood as being primarily an intellectual enterprise.

In designing a syllabus as well as conducting a class, teachers need to be conscious and deliberate about how they frame the central questions around which a course is organized, distinguish among levels of generality, establish rules of evidence, construct and compare interpretations that give information meaning, make productive connections between and among ideas and empirical phenomena, and design assignments to develop students' informed but critical stance toward assertions and claims. Such judgments constitute the intellectual core of the teacher's role in liberal education, and they cannot be abdicated to textbook publishers without severe risk. Good teaching is much more than a packaging and distributing function, and the intellectual side must be addressed explicitly.

There is general agreement about the need for teaching faculty's continuing intellectual vitality and development. Nevertheless, when one fully acknowledges the intellectual nature of good undergraduate teaching, it becomes clear that such vitality and development require a continuing program of writing and publishing to promote and express that vitality and development. In liberal education programs that aspire to promote students' capacities for independent, critical thinking and active intellectual involvement, faculty must continue to develop intellectually in a correspondingly active manner, one that goes beyond the passive notion of "keeping up with one's field." Active learning by faculty—the type of learning that will benefit their students—requires that faculty directly confront and perhaps extend or recast significant questions of their fields and that they submit ideas and arguments to peers for review and criticism. This last step, requiring author/teachers to respond to others' analyses and criticisms of their work, is crucial to the learning process.

The disciplined reflection involved in framing an argument, setting it in an appropriate context, developing it coherently, marshaling the necessary evidence, and demonstrating the argument's significance is a substantial learning experience for the author. Writing it down to communicate it effectively to others, without the ambiguities often tolerated in oral presentations, is in itself a vital part of thinking and learning. Does this sound familiar? Certainly it does, because this is precisely what most of us tell our students, and it is equally valid for faculty.

One's understanding of ideas is enhanced by participating in debates in the wider intellectual world and having to respond to the critical analyses of one's ideas by people detached from the immediate social network of the home institution. In addition, this activity is a powerful antidote to parochialism among an institution's faculty, a danger that has increased over the last decade as faculty turnover has declined.

This cluster of contributions to good teaching, realized through active scholarship, is augmented by other, perhaps less lofty but still significant contributions. For instance, one element of good teaching is to convince students to take intellectual risks, and in this the faculty's credibility is essential. We must practice what we preach, and this means demonstrating that the issues and ideas in our fields really are exciting and important and thus deserve the commitment of our own time and effort and the personal risks involved in explicitly advocating them to audiences outside of the local institution.

Moreover, an active program of writing enables faculty to stay in touch with the agonies their students go through in formulating and writing essays and receiving faculty criticism. Faculty who continue the struggle to hone their own writing skills are in a good position to give sound guidance to students about how to cast their argument, organize the sequence of its development, work from entire drafts or concentrate on sections, cite rather than reproduce descriptions, overcome dry spells, and maintain a sense of proportion about the whole enterprise. Faculty active in scholarship are more likely to be better at this than their colleagues who draw only on increasingly distant memories of graduate school experiences. Informed empathy and continually developing technical skills certainly enhance teaching effectiveness.

Finally, having an article accepted is a tangible expression that, in the judgment of disinterested professionals, the writer has something significant to say to other professionals. This recognition is virtually impossible for teachers to receive without publishing, and it is especially important in academia, where often faculty members will achieve the top rank of the profession (full professor) by the time they are in their forties. This means that, during the last 20 years or so of professional life, there are no more promotions or formal recognitions of achievement and value by the institution in which they teach. Active participation in scholarly debates, along with the sense of participation and of making a mark beyond the home campus, can help make individuals believe that their career is continuing to develop and go forward. This certainly will reduce the likelihood of burnout by ennui.

These are some of the ways in which scholarly publishing can contribute importantly to faculty morale, commitment, and confidence, all crucial to high-quality teaching.

Beyond Disciplinary Research

The pervasive belief that there is only one legitimate model of faculty scholarship—disciplinary research—is the second misconception that works against promoting scholarship by teaching faculty. Disciplinary research is only one type of faculty scholarship, a type whose agendas are set primarily by the work of faculty in research universities. It exerts a powerful hegemony throughout U.S. higher education, probably in good part through graduate school socialization and through the chronic emulation of research universities by upwardly mobile institutions. This hegemony is often strong even in institutions where faculty do little scholarship of any kind.

But conducting mainstream disciplinary research is difficult for most undergraduate faculty, who teach undergraduates in settings with heavy course loads and few research facilities and support services. The exclusive identification of faculty scholarship with disciplinary research, therefore, is a major source of the conclusion that scholarship and teaching are competitive activities.

Even in the case of disciplinary research, however, this is not strictly true, because there are a number of ways in which such research can be integrated into teaching responsibilities, to the benefit of all concerned.[3] And at the margins of disciplinary research, writing book reviews, survey articles, and teaching materials is more compatible with teaching and can be an effective vehicle for active faculty intellectual development. Reviews and surveys can be important in developing new knowledge, and they are frequently read by and useful to other teachers as well as to students. More teaching materials should be developed by teaching faculty, rather than by eminent researchers and teams of nonacademic writers organized by publishers, as is presently the case.

While disciplinary research should be supported and rewarded in undergraduate institutions, defining legitimate faculty scholarship in narrow terms works against productively expanding the scholarly enterprise. There are at least two additional types of scholarship that are valuable outlets for expressing and promoting the kind of active intellectual development necessary for good teaching.

First of all, there are innumerable fascinating and worthwhile research and publishing projects that are innovative by subject matter and by approach; valuable scholarship need not fit into conventional modes of disciplinary professionalism. Twenty or 30 years ago, it was difficult to find good outlets for publishing such work, but the creation and expansion of specialized journals focusing on issues such as the Third World, women, minorities, the environment, computers, cognitive science, and literary theory, to name just a few, now give faculty genuine opportunities to publish critical, heterodox scholarship and thus to engage in national debates significant to their intellectual lives, without having to conform to the canons of disciplinary research.

Writing and publishing about one's teaching is a second type of scholarship that is appropriate for teaching faculty but that lies outside disciplinary research. Analytical essays by teaching faculty, dealing with substantive and pedagogical issues arising directly out of the classroom and other instructional settings, is a genre that ought to be expanded and more fully developed. Following from the strongly intellectual nature of good teaching, the subjects especially needing to be addressed by such articles are the purposes, central questions, and themes around which courses and programs of study are or should be organized. For instance, is it still worthwhile in the social sciences to burden students with the full conceptual apparatus of Keynesian economics, or of functionalism, or of pluralism, or of behaviorism? If it is, how are these to be regarded in light of cogent criticisms and alternative ideas about how the social world develops and changes?

Essays on specific pedagogical strategies that support clearly defined educational goals are also important, and there are other features of the academy—such as advising, participatory governance, and faculty incentive structures—that affect teaching and learning and therefore warrant more public scrutiny and debate by teaching faculty. The type of writing about teaching I consider to be the most important, however, does not require faculty to become educational psychologists, a stance that easily leads to the tacit and damaging assumption that the content of teaching is fixed (e.g., Cross, 1986). Faculty should express their specialized expertise in addressing teaching. Review articles on textbooks can combine both aspects, because, after all, textbooks define and justify fundamental organizational conventions in respect to knowledge; engage or avoid key questions; establish rules of evidence; and contain decisions about emphases, sequence and pace of presentation, and the role of the teacher.

The personal consequences of morale and sense of accomplishment for faculty actively participating in, say, their disciplinary association's teaching caucus and writing about teaching may be more subtle and far-reaching than simple acknowledgment by others. The research-and-publication ethos in academic professionalism is so strong and pervasive that it is fair to deduce the existence of some—and perhaps considerable—anxiety and defensiveness among the vast majority of college faculty who do not write for publication (Finkelstein, 1984; Watkins, 1985). Writing about teaching, then, is a feasible means for faculty members to reduce value conflicts in their culture while remaining committed to teaching. By so doing, they heighten job satisfaction among nonresearching teachers.

It is clear that publishing about teaching, like all publishing, can widen personal networks of extra-institutional colleagues. What is less clear but no less important is that writing about teaching can serve to enlarge a teacher's circle of colleagues *within* one's home institution as well. Sending drafts of an article on teaching to faculty members in other departments is likely to be a more effective way to initiate colleagial relationships across disciplines than sending drafts of a research paper. Not only are undergraduate faculty substantially more specialized in their research than in their teaching, research papers' subjects, language, and conventions of evidence tend to be rather specific to each discipline. As opposed to disciplinary research, which often sets people apart even in the same discipline, faculty have much more in common in the rewards, frustrations, and even substance of their teaching. Finding new ways to expand one's network of colleagues within the campus, and thus the sources of intellectual stimulation and renewal, is especially important in conditions of low faculty turnover.

If faculty, as teachers, were to present more actively their ideas and experiences about the substance of their teaching in formal and public ways, it could encourage greater attention to the very real and vital intellectual dimensions of teaching, enhance job satisfaction, create opportunities for faculty to engage scholarly issues in a manner fully compatible with their teaching responsibilities, and thereby make curricula more educational and rewarding for teachers. All of these factors would contribute to better college and university teaching.

CONCLUDING REMARKS

The three higher education reports cited earlier (Boyer, 1987; Project on Redefining, 1985; Study Group, 1984) are in many respects excellent documents, full of sound educational ideas and enthusiasm about raising the quality of undergraduate education and the professional prestige of undergraduate teaching. In this effort, however, it is disappointing to find that they all fall back on the old shibboleth about teaching versus scholarship. When people and agencies closely identified with research universities and elite liberal arts colleges recommend that all others should eschew formal scholarship, it is extremely difficult not to sound patronizing.

The most important point, however, is that in making this analysis the reports' authors implicitly accept the tenet that teaching is not primarily an intellectual endeavor, that it is the transmission rather than the creation of knowledge. This conception of teaching, with its corresponding invidious distinction between "professional" development and "instructional" development, is itself one of the greatest obstacles to increasing the caliber of teaching and its professional recognition.

I have argued the contrary position that good teaching requires a consistent scholarly commitment on the part of faculty, a commitment that includes the formal presentation of ideas and findings for public scrutiny. The effort should not be to convince teaching faculty that they should not engage in scholarship, but rather that institutions serious about the undergraduate teaching enterprise should work imaginatively to make active scholarship compatible with teaching responsibilities. While faculty scholarship appropriate for undergraduate faculty will be different from that for faculty in research universities, in magnitude as well as in the range of acceptable types, the differences are properly seen as matters of degree.

10

Research on Writing About Teaching

In the last chapter, I argued that writing about one's teaching was a form of scholarship that should be promoted more strongly among college and university faculty, and especially among those who teach in institutions where disciplinary research is difficult. This does have a somewhat humorous aspect, echoing the old adage that, if one cannot do something, one could always teach about it. So what I am recommending is another layer: writing about teaching (while I am writing about writing about teaching).

Although alert to the ludicrous, I have looked into two dimensions of writing about teaching, in an effort to discover how such scholarship is seen in colleges and universities and to assess its substantive patterns. In 1982 and 1983, I conducted a survey and analyzed the contents of several college teaching journals, in both cases concentrating on the social sciences. My findings are the subject of this chapter.

THE PROFESSIONAL STATUS OF
WRITING ABOUT TEACHING

In conducting my survey, I sent questionnaires to the deans of social science or of liberal arts at 274 random selected four-year colleges and universities of various types, in order to determine the place of writing about teaching among social scientists at their institutions. Somewhat to my surprise, I received gracious and thoughtful replies from just under half of them. Table 10.1 shows the numbers and enrollments of all of the nation's four-year colleges and universities, arranged according to the Carnegie Council's (1976) classification of colleges and universities (described in Appendix A). Alongside these data are the respective rates of response to my questionnaire, by institutional category. My complete sample was 135 colleges and universities, or 9.8% of all four-year colleges and universities, representing a slightly larger proportion of all students enrolled in these institutions.

TABLE 10.1 Number and Enrollments of Four-Year Colleges and Universities (1982-1984) and Responses to Survey

Carnegie Foundation Category[a]	Institutions No.	%	Students No.[b]	%	Number of Questionnaires Sent	Returned
Research Universities	104	7.5	2,209	30.2	25	12
Doctoral Granting Univ.	109	7.9	1,220	16.7	19	10
Comprehensive C. & U. 1	424	30.7	2,971	40.6	78	47
Comprehensive C. & U. 2	171	12.4	332	4.5	42	16
Liberal Arts Colleges 1	142	10.2	214	2.9	31	12
Liberal Arts Colleges 2	430	31.2	370	5.0	79	38
TOTAL	1,380	100.0	7,316	100.0	274	135

[a]See Appendix A for a description of the Carnegie Foundation's classification scheme for colleges and universities.
[b]Number of students in thousands.
Source: Carnegie Foundation, 1987a.

Using the same Carnegie Council (1976) classification system, Table 10.2 presents the results from the survey. In constructing that table, I tabulated the responses from the survey by institutional type, faculty rank, type of institutional control (private versus public), and geographical region. As neither type of control nor region affected the results significantly, I dropped these variables in the reporting. (This is also true of the data presented later in Table 10.4).

It is no particular surprise to find, from the third question reported in Table 10.2, that respondents from research universities (RU) and liberal arts colleges 1 (LA 1) were the most definite about not encouraging faculty to write and publish about their teaching. The colleges in the Carnegie LA 1 category, so aptly called "university colleges" by Jencks and Riesman (1968), are the highly selective colleges that act as feeder schools for the graduate and professional schools of the most prestigious research universities. These colleges are among the most elite institutions of higher education, both in terms of social class and academic reputation, and they are full-fledged participants in the research university culture.

Moreover, on this same question, the table shows that the level of encouragement for faculty writing about teaching is also not overwhelming in comprehensive universities and colleges (CUC 1 and 2), either. From the answers to the fourth question, however, it is clear that CUC 1 and 2 institutions give substantially greater weight to this

TABLE 10.2 Deans' Responses to Questionnaire

	% of Respondents per Institution Type[a]						
	RU	DG	CUC1	CUC2	LA1	LA2	ALL
1. Have formal faculty development program	67	70	47	73	50	61	57
2. Social science faculty write about teaching:							
Frequently	--	--	11	--	--	3	4
Never	--	--	11	7	33	16	12
3. Faculty writing about teaching is:							
Definitely encouraged	--	10	15	7	--	3	7
Definitely not encouraged	83	50	60	80	83	68	67
4. Publication about teaching is strong evidence of professional development	8	30	51	80	12	18	40
5. Administrators consider such writing and publishing to be more important than do social science departments	25	20	15	--	--	16	14
6. Social science departments value such writing and publishing less than do other academic departments	17	30	21	--	8	--	12
7. Importance of such writing in the last decade:							
Increased	25	40	30	27	17	26	27
Declined	8	20	2	7	--	--	12
Declined relative to disciplinary research	8	--	11	13	17	13	4
8. Importance of such writing in the next decade:							
Will increase	25	10	30	33	8	29	26
Will decline	8	20	2	--	--	--	4
Will decline relative to disciplinary research	8	10	9	13	8	13	10

[a]The percentages of responses to each question do not add up to 100 because I present only the categories of answers that are the most interesting. The modal response to many questions was "no change," "equal," or an indefinite "yes and no," "maybe," or "possibly." See Appendix A for a description of the Carnegie Foundation's classification scheme for colleges and universities.

form of scholarship in reviewing a faculty member's record for purposes of promotion and tenure than do RU or LA 1 institutions.

It is fair to infer, then, that the lack of active support for writing about teaching stems from different sources in different types of institutions. In RU and LA 1, ignoring such scholarship no doubt is an expression of a very strong commitment to disciplinary research as *the* legitimate form of faculty scholarship. On the other hand, comments on several questionnaires from respondents from LA 2 institutions suggest a very different reason. These colleges' apparent lack of interest in faculty writing about teaching appears to stem, in good part, from their attaching but little importance to faculty scholarship in general. Finally, several respondents, most notably from the RU and DG categories, said that writing about teaching would be favorably viewed as evidence of teaching commitment.

Regarding the fifth question in Table 10.2, most respondents from all institutions saw little difference in the value given to writing about teaching among various levels and units within their institutions. When there was a difference, usually administrators supported writing more strongly than did faculty, and social scientists tended to be less interested than are faculty from other departments. This last point was blurred a bit by occasional references on the questionnaires to the high value that education faculty put on writing about teaching. This, of course, was not what I had in mind when I asked the question. (And it raises the specter of writing about teaching about teaching.)

There is considerable dispersion in the responses to all the questions from the heterogeneous DG category, but the relatively positive attitude of several of them toward writing about teaching is worth mentioning. For one thing, it helps to offset the image that the universities in this category are uniformly struggling to move "up" a notch and achieve RU status by means of slavish emulation.

Finally, in the responses to the seventh and eighth questions, there is evidence of substantial sentiment in CUC 1, CUC 2, and LA 2 that writing about teaching has become more important during the last decade and will become even more important in the coming decade. While this is heartening, it also is part of a very uneven pattern of responses from institutions in the three groups. In the case of LA 2, their perception of this scholarly activity's increasing importance coexists uneasily with reports that little value is attached to it at the time of faculty review and that it is not encouraged. This lack of encouragement of scholarship in general and writing about teaching in particular—even though nearly two-thirds of them said that their institutions had formal faculty development programs—is consistent with my characterization of faculty development programs in the first part of Chapter 9.

The seeming inconsistency among CUC 1 and CUC 2 institutions is even more striking. Again there is the perception of the increasing importance of this form of faculty scholarship, the substantial presence of faculty development programs, and little or no effort to promote such work among the faculty. But a large proportion of these institutions report that it is valued highly as a form of professional development! There is the hope, of course (and a hope supported by a couple of comments written on questionnaires), that the survey itself might have stimulated some effort to encourage faculty to regard the intellectual aspects of their teaching as subjects worth writing about.

SOCIAL SCIENCE TEACHING JOURNALS

The second investigation I undertook regarding writing about teaching was to read the articles that appeared in five leading social science teaching journals from 1978 to 1983. The journals I reviewed are *History Teacher, Journal of Economic Education, Teaching of Psychology, Teaching Political Science,* and *Teaching Sociology.* Table 10.3 lists some background information on these journals, based on two representative issues. Table 10.4 cross-classifies the authors of each journal's articles by academic rank (when available) and institutional type, and it lists editorial board members by the types of institution with which they are affiliated.

It is clear that the composition of the journals' authors and editorial board memberships are rather different, reflecting in part each journal's own history and the particular people and agencies involved in that history. For instance, *Teaching of Psychology* is the only one of the five journals that is published under the direct auspices of a national disciplinary association. This gives it greater visibility within the disci-

TABLE 10.3 Information on Social Science Teaching Journals Surveyed

| Journal | Date Begun | Publisher | Circu- lation | Total pages | Representative Issues[a] | | | |
| | | | | | Articles | | Book Reviews | |
					No.	pp/art.	No.	pp/rev.
History Teacher	1967	Soc. for Hist. of Ed.	2,500	286	13	14.8	71	1.0
J. of Economics Education	1969	Heldref	1,150	158	17	8.6	2	2.5
Teaching of Psychology	1974	Amer. Psychol. Association	3,200	297	43	2.4	3	2.0
Teaching Political Science	1973	Heldref	600	83	11	5.4	8	1.8
Teaching Sociology	1973	Sage	900	235	14	15.9	--	--

[a]Combined Information from two representative issues.

TABLE 10.4 Surveyed Journals Author and Editorial Board Member Affiliations

	Institution Type[a]						For-eign	Nonaca-demic	Total
	RU	DG CUC1	CUC2	LA1	LA2	CC			
History Teacher									
Ass't Professors	8	4 2	--	2	--	--	--	--	15
Assoc. Professors	11	6 5	--	6	--	--	--	--	28
Professors	15	8 5	1	1	--	--	--	--	30
Not Available	4	1 1	--	1	--	5	5	10	27
TOTAL AUTHORS	38	19 12	1	9	--	5	5	10	100
Ed. Board Members	29	7 29	--	4	4	7	--	21	100
Journal of Economics Education									
Ass't Professors	5	3 2	--	--	--	--	--	--	10
Assoc. Professors	5	18 10	--	--	--	--	--	--	32
Professors	13	10 13	--	--	--	--	--	--	36
Not Available	7	3 2	--	--	--	4	8	--	23
TOTAL AUTHORS	29	34 26	--	--	--	4	8	--	100
Ed. Board Members[b]	78	-- 11	--	--	--	--	--	11	100
Teaching of Psychology									
TOTAL AUTHORS	42	13 24	2	6	2	2	4	5	100
Ed. Board Members	16	11 37	21	11	--	--	--	3	100
Teaching Political Science									
Ass't Professors	8	9 12	1	--	1	--	--	--	30
Assoc. Professors	5	7 11	1	3	--	--	--	--	27
Professors	5	3 5	2	2	1	--	--	--	17
Not Available	3	4 2	--	--	1	2	6	9	26
TOTAL AUTHORS	21	23 29	4	5	2	2	6	9	100
Ed. Board Members	33	17 8	--	8	8	--	8	17	100
Teaching Sociology									
Ass't Professors	7	4 6	2	2	1	--	--	--	21
Assoc. Professors	13	4 11	3	3	--	--	--	--	34
Professors	10	5 5	1	2	--	--	--	--	24
Not Available	7	5 3	1	--	1	2	3	1	22
TOTAL AUTHORS	37	18 25	6	7	1	2	3	1	100
Ed. Board Members	38	25 8	4	4	4	8	--	9	100

[a]Each number in the table is a percentage of the total number of the journal's authors or editorial board members.

[b]Two editorial board members of the *Journal of Economics Education* could not be identified by institutional affiliation and were not counted in the percentages.

Note: See Appendix A for a description of the Carnegie Foundation's classification scheme for colleges and universities (RU, DG, CUC1, CUC2, LA1, LA2).

pline and probably accounts for the greater range of institutional types from which its authors are drawn. At the same time, perhaps the relatively small proportion of its editorial board members from the RU category is a result of less need to legitimize the journal with eminent scholars on the board. Sponsorship by the disciplinary association, however, also means virtually instant professional prestige, and the high proportion of the journal's authors from RU undoubtedly reflects this.

Table 10.4 shows the strong representation of authors from the largest institutions with significant graduate schools (RU and DG) and from elite private liberal arts colleges (LA 1) in all of the journals (except *Teaching Political Science*), a presence that is particularly notable since those three types of institutions reported such weak incentives for writing of this kind. It is especially intriguing that the representation of assistant professors from these three institutional types is as great as or greater than the proportions of assistant professors among the authors from CUC 1 and 2 and LA 2.

CUC 1 faculty are a definite presence as authors in all five journals, but their presence is not as large as one might expect either from their quantitative importance among national college and university faculty or from what appear to be incentives for this type of professional activity at CUC 1. And faculty from CUC 2 and LA 2 are definitely underrepresented. The entire pattern is no doubt a particular expression of the penchant of highly professionalized RU, DG, and LA 1 faculty to write and publish in general, supported by their greater opportunities provided by their employing institutions (such as teaching loads, libraries, clerical support, and so on).

But the differences among the journals are more striking than the commonalities. For instance, I have already noted the special status of *Teaching of Psychology* and some of its implications. The large percentage of *Journal of Economic Education* authors who are from DG is distinctive, as is the pattern of authors' faculty ranks in *Teaching Political Science* and, to a lesser extent, *Teaching Sociology*, which are less top heavy in respect to the seniority of the authors' faculty ranks than is the case of the other four journals.

Let us turn now to Table 10.5, where the major categories of the journal articles' contents over 5 years are presented. As the note at the bottom of the table states, the percentages look a bit odd because a particular article may be entered in several categories or in only one. Classification was made more difficult because of some author vagueness that was not rectified by the editors. For example, many of the articles about courses did not state the course's level and prerequisites or whether it was designed for majors, nonmajors, or whomever.

TABLE 10.5 Characteristics of Articles in Five Social Science Teaching Journals, 1978-1983

	History Teacher	J. of Econ. Ed.	Teaching of Psychol.	Teaching Pol. Sci.	Teaching Sociology
TOTAL NUMBER OF ARTICLES	144	48	206	165	140
LEVEL OF TEACHING:[a]					
Primary and Second.	23	6	1	--	--
College and University:	34	46	48	42	59
Lower Division	11	40	26	11	34
Upper Division	20	2	16	6	4
Major	--	2	9	2	3
Graduate	3	2	5	6	3
SUBJECTS OF ARTICLES:[a]					
Pedagogical Techniques and Evaluation	22	63	55	50	63
New Content:	31	--	9	13	14
Women	7	--	--	6	3
Minorities in U.S.	2	--	--	1	1
Africa, Asia, & Lat. Am.	12	--	--	1	1
Quantitative Methods	2	--	--	4	5
Teaching Materials	24	--	7	8	9
Student Characteristics	2	17	14	6	11
Teaching Profession	6	10	7	5	6
Nature of Discipline	10	--	4	10	6
Institutional Context	--	--	2	1	2

[a]Each number is a percentage of total articles in the journal, but the categories are neither exhaustive nor mutually exclusive.

Looking farther down the table, the relative lack of attention to quantitative methods is surprising, even though it corroborates my claim in Chapter 8 about the lack of attention to statistics teaching. There is national concern about college students' quantitative abilities. Some of the disciplines represented by the journals, such as economics and psychology, are highly quantitative; political science and sociology also have strongly quantitative aspects; and one would think that the controversy over the use of statistics by those working in the vineyard of the "new social history" would have stimulated more attention to this area by authors and editors of *History Teacher.*

The articles whose subject was pedagogical techniques and evaluation did not regard teaching content to be an issue and were devoted to different pedagogical methods for getting (implicitly) conventional content across to students and assessing the effectiveness of that teaching method. In contrast, the articles dealing specifically with new content argued that ground-breaking information or questions should supplement or supplant the usual fare.

The proportion of each journal's articles addressing new content probably has the same ordinal relation as the way one would rank the five social science disciplines according to the degree of internal consensus about each discipline's definition. That is, economists (even after the stagflation of the mid-1970s) are the most confident about what constitutes the questions, subject matter, and methods of their discipline. They are followed by psychologists, political scientists, and sociologists, with historians being the least ready to draw lines that determine what does and does not fall within their professional purview. Except for the transposition of political science and sociology, the same disciplinary ordering is apparent under the "nature of discipline" category, where reflections on this issue are called for relatively infrequently.[1]

CONCLUDING REMARKS

It is clear from these brief surveys that there are at least two major types of effort to be made in order to make writing about teaching a more important form of faculty scholarship. I will begin with the lack of visibility of this kind of scholarship, especially among faculty teaching in institutions not strongly oriented toward regular disciplinary research. It is ironic that, at least among the five journals I surveyed, there evidently is no visibility problem of such scholarship among faculty teaching at institutions, such as research universities, where it is not highly valued nor presumed likely to become so.

On the other hand, from the testimony of deans and from the composition of authorship, there is but slight encouragement for and engagement in such writing by faculty at institutions where they actually do more teaching, where writing about teaching is valued more highly, and where this type of faculty scholarship would be a feasible and productive alternative to disciplinary research.

So, more effort at promoting this form of scholarship among these faculty is in order, but just what kind of writing about teaching would be desirable? Here is the second major area of needed work: stressing the importance of the *intellectual* side of our teaching through this literature. As noted in the previous chapter, I have no intention of disparaging the importance of pedagogical technique and evaluation. Research and improvements in both areas are essential, and these are the issues that appear to be the principal interest of most of those directly involved in the nascent academic discipline of higher education.

Nevertheless, if the literature on college and university teaching in all disciplines were to continue to be dominated by technique and evaluation studies, pressing questions about teaching content would continue to be relegated to a second order of importance. Not only are these content questions vitally important for teaching faculty to engage and debate, their subordination to teaching methods would reinforce existing convictions that teaching is merely a transmission function or, as I have referred to it earlier, a packaging and distributing function.

This is precisely the stance toward teaching that serves to denigrate the intellectual side of teaching, and thus to disparage its status in disciplinary professionalism. As I have noted, the idea that the content of teaching is fixed, beyond the capacity and responsibility of teaching faculty to affect significantly, implies that the major questions about teaching are the effectiveness of different types of presentations. This leads to the prescription that faculty's writing about teaching is properly limited to assessment and lies essentially in the realm of educational psychology (e.g., Cross, 1986), rather than in the faculty member's academic discipline.

This conception of teaching, buttressed by the contents of the five social science journals I surveyed, also strengthens existing hierarchies among faculties and institutions and does a serious disservice to our students by restricting the potential of a promising avenue of faculty vitality and educational improvement. As I have suggested, bringing substantive questions to the fore is easier in some disciplines than it is in others, but it is an effort worth making.

PART III
Beyond the Curriculum

11

Whither Black Public Colleges and Universities? A Review of Institutional Options

The consistent theme of the preceding chapters of this book has been the improvement of undergraduate liberal education, and I have advocated for critical-inquiry education as especially promising. This approach entails a pedagogy that directly and plausibly encourages the development of habits of mind to which all liberal education pays lip service but all too often discourages in practice.

While I have spoken about democratic education in many of those chapters, it has been democratic education in terms of content and pedagogy. As I have argued, critical, independent thinking and other habits of mind related to critical-inquiry education directly contribute to good democratic citizenship, the encouragement of which should be seen as one of the broader goals of undergraduate education. Nevertheless, there are other conditions, beyond the curricular and pedagogical, that are necessary for colleges and universities to be able to support and enhance democratic citizenship. Among these, the availability of higher education to all who can benefit from it is extremely important.

The critical questions, from this vantage point, are who will be able to reap the multiple benefits from attending colleges and universities, and who will be excluded? That is, instead of regarding democratic education as a process in which both substance and pedagogy educate students in democratic principles and practices, another side of democratic education is the availability of quality higher education for all capable of benefiting from it. Democratic education can be seen as meaningful *access* to higher education for as wide a spectrum of students as is feasible.

This chapter analyzes the situation of a set of institutions that are outstanding in regard to their role as democratic access institutions. These are the public colleges and universities that historically have provided access to higher education for generations of black Americans, so poorly served in educational services. These institutions have had a clear identity as caste institutions (following Bullock, 1967; Drake, 1955; McPherson, 1974; and Rudolph, 1962), an identity imposed on them by the coercive powers of the state. Now these institutions need to make deliberate choices about redefining their place in U.S. higher education, which for them is a system that suddenly has very new rules and parameters, possibilities and dangers. These colleges and universities are outstanding democratic institutions, and their role in providing democratic access, in addition to its intrinsic importance, makes the story extremely important for the system of higher education as a whole.

WATERSHED CHANGES

Nineteen states and the District of Columbia have public colleges and universities that have historically served black students (see Table 11.1). In fact, as part of the segregated societies of the U.S. South, until two or three decades ago they were the only public colleges and universities that enrolled blacks in most of these places. The landmark U.S. Supreme Court case of *Brown vs. Board of Education* in 1954, as well as the *Adams* series of litigations of the early 1970s, forced the previously all-white colleges and universities in these states to admit black students, albeit frequently only after violent confrontations with the federal government. The *Adams* case has been interpreted to include the integration of black institutions as well, and many white students have enrolled in some historically black institutions. Even with these shifts in enrollment, however, historically black schools still awarded, relative to their share of enrollments, disproportionate numbers of baccalaureate degrees to black Americans in the early 1980s.

The previously all-white colleges and universities that only two or three decades ago shunned black students—to the extent of denying them the right even to visit the campus or to compete against their athletic teams—not only enroll black students, but actively recruit them. This certainly does not mean that life on white campuses is easy or pleasant for black students, but the large numbers of black students choosing to attend previously all-white colleges and universities have led to considerable uncertainty about the educational roles of public black colleges and universities. This uncertainty is exceedingly serious, and potentially fatal, in an era of declining numbers of 18–22 year olds

TABLE 11.1 Enrollments at Historically Black Public Colleges and Universities

STATE/School	%of Fall 1986 Enrollment				
	Black	Latino	White	Foreign	TOTAL
ALABAMA:					
Alabama A & M University	72	0	11	17	3,928
Alabama State University	98	0	1	2	3,540
ARKANSAS: Univ. of Arkansas, Pine Bluff	80	0	20	1	2,921
DELAWARE: Delaware State College	54	1	43	2	2,327
DISTRICT OF COLUMBIA: University of D.C.	89	2	5	0	11,098
FLORIDA: Florida A & M University	82	2	13	3	5,411
GEORGIA:					
Albany State College	81	0	18	1	1,902
Fort Valley State College	91	0	7	2	1,811
Savannah State College	78	0	18	4	1,694
KENTUCKY: Kentucky State University	41	0	58	1	2,205
LOUISIANA:					
Grambling State University	95	0	1	3	5,224
Southern University A & M College	90	0	3	6	9,170
Southern University, New Orleans	87	1	8	5	3,302
MARYLAND:					
Bowie State University	59	1	33	6	2,867
Coppin State University	88	0	4	4	2,315
Morgan State University	86	0	5	9	3,752
University of Maryland—Eastern Shore	71	1	23	4	1,331
MISSISSIPPI:					
Alcorn State University	91	0	9	0	2,329
Jackson State University	93	0	2	5	6,319
Mississippi Valley State University	100	0	0	0	2,002
MISSOURI: Lincoln University	31	0	64	3	2,486
NORTH CAROLINA:					
Elizabeth City State University	82	0	17	1	1,613
Fayetteville State University	74	1	23	0	2,921
North Carolina A & T State University	83	0	12	4	5,966
North Carolina Central University	81	0	17	1	5,040
Winston-Salem State University	84	0	15	0	2,590
OHIO: Central State University	79	0	14	7	2,424
OKLAHOMA: Langston University	51	1	38	7	1,901
PENNSYLVANIA:					
Cheyney State University	95	1	3	1	1,507
Lincoln University	89	1	8	2	1,245
SOUTH CAROLINA: South Carolina State Coll.	92	0	7	1	3,869
TENNESSEE: Tennessee State University	63	0	32	3	6,739
TEXAS:					
Prairie View A & M University	81	1	9	8	4,499
Texas Southern University	74	4	3	19	7,249
VIRGINIA:					
Norfolk State University	85	0	12	3	7,458
Virginia State University	86	0	12	2	3,583
WEST VIRGINIA:					
Bluefield State College	8	0	91	1	2,593
West Virginia State College	12	0	87	1	4,383

Source: The Chronicle of Higher Education, 34 (43) (July 6, 1988), pp. A20-A29.

and heightened interinstitutional competition for students. These schools are forced into redefining their missions and purposes so as to serve students effectively and to create a secure niche for themselves in their state systems of higher education. Their principal alternatives include shifting their emphasis to one or more of the following functions and corresponding institutional models:

1. A comprehensive public institution serving the entire population of a particular region or urban area
2. An academically specialized institution emphasizing a set of specialized programs
3. A comprehensive public institution that, while significantly integrated, retains its identity as an institution especially (but not exclusively) committed to and appropriate for serving black students and communities.

These models are certainly not mutually exclusive. They are matters of degree but very important matters of degree. The choices a particular historically black college or university has made and is making depend on its unique circumstances, including resources and setting. The purpose of this chapter, then, is to outline some of the prospects and problems involved in taking any of these directions.

GENERAL-PURPOSE REGIONAL UNIVERSITY

At first glance, the most obvious route for a historically black college or university might seem to become a general, racially neutral regional state institution, with its mix of professional and liberal arts programs primarily serving area students. Colleges and universities of this type, which are usually found in the Carnegie Foundation's category entitled "Comprehensive Universities and Colleges" (see Appendix A) are vulnerable to the criticism that their missions have not been specified in precise and distinctive ways (e.g., Dunham, 1969; Weathersby, 1984). Nevertheless, the regional state college and university is a form of institutional identity that has proven to be acceptable both to students and to state legislatures.

Lincoln University in Missouri and both of the historically black colleges and universities in West Virginia are located some distance away from other public colleges and have already become regional campuses to the extent that black students do not comprise the major-

ity of their enrollments. In fact, black Americans are very small proportions of total enrollment in both of the West Virginia institutions.

Most students at the University of Arkansas at Pine Bluff, Dela-
ware State College, the University of the District of Columbia, and
South Carolina State University are black, but these four colleges and
universities do not have nearby competing public institutions and thus
have considerable potential for becoming general regional or urban
institutions in their state higher education systems. Some of the tensions associated with this model are illustrated by Fort Valley State
College in Georgia, which has been under substantial pressure from
the local white community to adopt this new identity more quickly
than the college has been willing or able to do (Bellamy, 1983).

One of the obvious shortcomings of this model is very well cap-
tured by the remarks made in 1970, during the landmark *Adams*
litigation, by Dr. Andrew Billingsley, former president of Morgan
State University in Maryland. Referring to the NAACP Legal Defense
Fund, which was suing to integrate both black and white colleges and
universities, Dr. Billingsley stated that, "They have a conception of
integration—of desegregation—which requires a white majority and
requires Black Americans always to be in the minority" (quoted in T.
Brown, 1983, p. 5). What this regional state college model means for
black institutions and black students, then, is white control and cultural
dominance in institutions that formerly offered some space for a black
control and culture. The extent to which these black colleges and
universities have been able to perform this role, of course, has been
severely constrained, but the potential is there, and the regional state
college model casts doubt on it ever being realized.

Even if this model were universally attractive, however, it is not
available to all historically black colleges and universities. As already
suggested, spatial factors—the racial geography of an institution's location and its distance from potential competition—are critical in an
individual institution's ability to achieve the status of a regional institution. Many historically black colleges and universities, however, have
severe disadvantages in this respect.

Because public black colleges were founded during the period of
formal racial segregation, their proximity to white institutions was not
considered to be especially important. Since colleges and universities
did not compete for students across racial lines, black colleges were
frequently located alongside white institutions, and white institutions
often were opened very near already operating historically black
colleges and universities. Table 11.2 presents nine examples of such

TABLE 11.2 Enrollments for Neighboring Historically Black Institutions and White Institutions Established before 1954

STATE/School	Date est.	% of Fall 1986 Enrollment			TOTAL
		Black	Latino	White	
ALABAMA:					
Alabama A & M University	1875	72	0	11	3,928
University of Alabama, Huntsville[a]	1950	7	1	90	6,161
FLORIDA:					
Florida A & M University	1887	82	2	13	5,411
Florida State University[a]	1851	7	3	86	22,990
KENTUCKY:					
Kentucky State University	1886	41	0	58	2,205
University of Kentucky[a]	1865	3	1	93	20,692
LOUISIANA:					
Southern University A & M College	1880	90	0	3	9,170
Louisiana State University[a]	1860	7	2	83	28,421
MARYLAND:					
University of Maryland - Eastern Shore	1886	71	1	23	1,331
Salisbury State College[a]	1925	6	1	92	4,708
OKLAHOMA:					
Langston University	1897	51	1	38	1,901
Oklahoma State University[a]	1890	3	1	85	21,676
PENNSYLVANIA:					
Cheyney State University	1837	95	1	3	1,507
West Chester Univ. of Pennsylvania[a]	1812	6	1	91	10,498
TEXAS:					
Texas Southern University	1947	74	4	3	7,249
University of Houston[a]	1927	7	7	71	28,164
VIRGINIA:					
Norfolk State University	1935	85	0	12	7,458
Old Dominion University[a]	1930	10	1	84	15,463

[a]Previously all-white institutions.

Source: The Chronicle of Higher Education, 34 (43) (July 6, 1988), pp. A20-A29.

propinquity effected before 1954, which was the beginning of the end of legal segregation in education. These historically black colleges and universities, lacking a clearly defined service area, are seriously handicapped in becoming recognized as general, regionally based institutions. The disproportionate expansion of the previously all-white institutions relative to the nearby historically black colleges and universities during the 1960s and early 1970s illustrates this quite tangibly.

These locational disadvantages, however, are not just a legacy of legal segregation. Public higher education systems in the states with historically black colleges and universities expanded during the boom years of the 1960s and early 1970s, not only by the growth of existing campuses. The states also opened new campuses, and Table 11.3 lists eight examples of new public institutions, which were parts of the state systems historically identified as all-white, and were established near historically black colleges and universities *after the end of legal racial segregation in education.*[1] This action was a clear signal that at least 10 historically black colleges and universities were going to have a very difficult time getting recognized as regional campuses by state authorities.

The case of the University of Tennessee at Nashville, however, shows that such actions are not necessarily irrevocable. Beginning as an extension center in 1947 and later becoming an all-white two-year

TABLE 11.3 Enrollments for Neighboring Historically Black Institutions and White Institutions Established after 1954

STATE/School	Date est.	% of Fall 1986 Enrollment			TOTAL
		Black	Latino	White	
ALABAMA:					
Alabama State University	1874	98	0	1	3,540
Auburn University at Montgomery[a]	1967	14	0	85	5,183
GEORGIA:					
Savannah State College	1890	78	0	18	1,694
Armstrong State College[a]	1964[b]	14	0	83	2,732
LOUISIANA:					
Grambling State University	1901	95	0	1	5,224
LA State University, Shreveport[a]	1972	8	1	89	4,152
Southern University at New Orleans	1956	87	1	8	3,302
University of New Orleans[a]	1958	16	5	74	16,083
MARYLAND:					
Coppin State University		88	0	4	2,315
Morgan State University		86	0	5	3,752
Univ. of Maryland, Baltimore County[a]	1966	12	1	78	9,267
NORTH CAROLINA:					
North Carolina A & T State University		83	0	12	5,966
Winston-Salem State University		84	0	15	2,590
Univ. of North Carolina, Greensboro[a]	1961[b]	10	0	87	10,696
OHIO:					
Central State University[c]	1884	79	0	14	2,424
Wright State University[a]	1964	6	1	91	16,075
VIRGINIA:					
Virginia State University	1882	86	0	12	3,583
Virginia Commonwealth University[a]	1965	14	1	82	19,641

[a]Institutions of previously all-white systems.
[b]The year established as a comprehensive, 4-year, coeducational institution.
[c]1982 enrollment figures.
Source: The Chronicle of Higher Education, 34 (43) (July 6, 1988), pp. A20-A29.

college, in 1971 it was made into a four-year comprehensive institution. As such, it directly competed with historically black Tennessee State University, also in Nashville. But, by a 1977 court order, the University of Tennessee at Nashville was merged *into* neighboring black Tennessee State University (Shannon, 1982; Shimeall, 1980).

Placing new campuses for whites near campuses for blacks is not unique to states with historically black colleges and universities. Table 11.4 shows that similar decisions about location were made in some large northern cities where there were significant concentrations of black populations and no historically black colleges and universities. In these situations, a new branch campus of the flagship state university was opened in a city already served by a state college. The university branch, with its greater prestige and per-student academic resources, and higher admissions requirements, offered opportunities for local middle-class white students to attend a public institution that had substantially smaller proportions of black (and working-class) students than the state college. The new campuses, therefore, drew off much of the growth of the respective city's college enrollment and became virtually white institutions, while the older campuses became predominantly black. Astin (1982) provides an excellent discussion of the need to put meaning into "equal access."

The University of Illinois at Chicago (formerly Chicago Circle) is the prime example of the effects of such an action on racial composition of institutional enrollment. Although less dramatic, the pattern is still evident in the cases of the SUNY College at Buffalo and SUNY at

TABLE 11.4 Enrollments for Selected Urban Colleges and Universities

STATE/School	Date est.	% of Fall 1986 Enrollment			TOTAL
		Black	Latino	White	
ILLINOIS:					
Chicago State University	1869	83	2	12	7,763
University of Illinois at Chicago	1965	10	8	67	25,330
MICHIGAN:					
Wayne State University	1864	22	2	69	28,764
University of Michigan, Dearborn	1971	6	2	89	7,120
MISSOURI:					
Harris-Stowe State College	1857	72	0	25	1,374
University of Missouri, St. Louis	1963	9	1	88	12,328
NEW YORK:					
SUNY College at Buffalo	1871	8	2	88	12,011
SUNY at Buffalo	1962	5	2	82	23,977

Source: The Chronicle of Higher Education, 34 (43) (July 6, 1988), pp. A20-A29.

Buffalo, even though the socioeconomic differences in student bodies are expressed only marginally in racial terms. It is also true of Boston State College, which was closed 16 years after the opening of the University of Massachusetts at Boston in 1965.

The major point here has been to demonstrate the difficulties facing over half of the public historically black colleges and universities in gaining the status of general-purpose regional institutions, whether or not this is considered to be a desirable model.

ACADEMICALLY SPECIALIZED INSTITUTIONS

A second possible way for a historically black college or university to secure a valued place for itself in its state system of higher education is by developing its strengths in particular curricular areas and becoming a preferred institution for students studying a particular field or desiring to participate in a special program. In cases where this would entail building on prior strengths, agriculture and education are two fields that might be feasible for some black colleges and universities.[3]

Technical and vocational education, and special programs for underprepared students—two additional areas frequently mentioned in considering the future role of historically black colleges and universities—might also hold promise. These were supposedly the historical functions of black institutions, when they were operating under strict segregation; the low level of occupational aspiration embodied in technical education and the taint of intellectual inferiority in remedial programs was at that time deemed right and proper for colleges serving blacks. It is clear, however, that the second-class academic citizenship resulting from this type of institutional identification would inevitably have undesirable racial overtones.

This is emphasized in Bullock (1967) and Peeps (1981), which are historical studies of the educational "detour" represented by channeling black colleges into noncollegiate forms of technical and vocational training. The range of conclusions on this issue can be appreciated by looking at the recommendations of the Carnegie Commission (1971), which sees real advantages for historically black institutions to develop such specializations, while Lincoln (1971) argues vehemently that this should not happen. For studies of the current operation of remedial education in historically black colleges and universities, see Ningard (1982) and Berrian (1982).

In addition to the drawback of implicitly linking remedial and technical education with race, there is a likely market problem in respect to such institutional specialization. In the last three decades, both areas of instruction have become the explicit provinces of public community colleges in most locales.

This market aspect, with the entry of the public community colleges, may have been part of the reason for the definite drift from specialized to general institutions throughout the nation. Many and probably most of the polytechnic institutes, teachers' colleges, A & M colleges, and other publicly supported, specialized postsecondary educational institutions have gradually and not so gradually drifted toward the form of a more general-purpose college and university. This tendency was apparent before World War II, but it has accelerated in the last 40 years.

There is more to it than supply-side considerations, however. As Jencks and Riesman (1968) argue, there is a powerful push exerted by notions of academic status that propels colleges and universities in the direction of expanding their mission to include the liberal arts. Faculty and administrators, deeply influenced by professional socialization and peer pressure, feel this push strongly, but it also registers in the student market. Many students prefer to go to a multipurpose college or university to pursue courses of study for which there are good specialized institutions.

These are some of the difficulties in maintaining an academically specialized identity, and their magnitude should not be underestimated.

One avenue by which institutional divisions of labor may come about is illustrated by the response of Georgia's higher education authorities to court-ordered desegregation of the two state colleges in Savannah. In the early 1980s, the School of Education at Savannah State College, the black institution, was moved to the neighboring white Armstrong State College; in return, Savannah State received Armstrong State's School of Business. This was a wholesale swap, including faculty, students, and equipment. A similar arrangement has been considered by the U.S. Department of Justice in its negotiations with Alabama state authorities in respect to Alabama State University and Alabama A & M ("U.S. Suggests Settlement," 1985).

BLACK-ORIENTED MULTIRACIAL INSTITUTIONS

The third possibility considered here is for a historically black public college or university to maintain a primary commitment to the education of black students and service to black communities, while effectively meeting the educational needs of substantial numbers of white students.[4]

In many respects the arguments for explicitly asserting a transformed version of the traditional mission of the historically black public college or university are compelling, but there are also substantial difficulties associated with this approach, whether it is pursued in its own right or in conjunction with the regional or academic-specialization model. Its success depends on the ability of an institution's faculty and administrators to convince students, state governing boards, and state legislatures that sustaining a black identity is consistent with high academic quality. This must be done at the same time that the schools are struggling to overcome the severe disadvantages imposed on them because of their identity as black institutions, a legacy of the time in which they were caste institutions.

A variant of this strategy would be to redefine an institution's central mission more broadly. Rather than being dedicated specifically to the education of blacks, it might orient its purpose to the education of minority students more generally, a definition that could also include foreign students from Africa, Asia, and Latin America. While the data in Table 11.1 show that foreign student enrollments are substantial in a few historically black colleges and universities, they also suggest that historically black colleges and universities are not especially attractive to nonforeign Latino students. (The numbers of Asian and Native American student enrollments, although not listed in the table, are also small and not encouraging.)

Among minority students, emphasizing programs and services appropriate for Latino students might hold the greatest promise, because of both their numbers in the general population and the inhospitality of most four-year colleges toward them (Astin, 1982; Hodgkinson, 1983; Webster, 1984). A curricular emphasis on international relations and business, especially with African, Caribbean, and Latin American nations, might well be an effective strategy for attracting Latino and black students. Such programs could stress some of the common historical experiences of the two groups and serve the nation by preparing minority students for careers in international affairs, a badly needed service (President's Commission, 1979; Stent, 1984). In the same vein, emphasizing the education of teachers specifically prepared to work with black and Latino children might also be attractive to students, faculty, and legislators.

An institution's internal and external political climate is probably more critical for successfully developing along these lines than for developing either as a comprehensive regional school or as an academically specialized institution (Cook, 1978; Davis, 1981; Godwin, 1971; J. Williams, 1984). Among other problems, an institution may be dismayed to find that it has some undesirable allies in these efforts, allies who are eager to recreate a dual system of higher education in which institutions that serve black or minority students constitute the lowest tier.

SCHOLARSHIP AND ACADEMIC MATTERS

As I have stressed throughout this chapter, the new type of institutional identification that will be found to be feasible for a particular historically black college or university depends on local circumstances, which will produce diversity within each of the general models. What is common to all such successful redefinitions of institutional missions and purposes, however, is the need for significant curricular revisions and supporting forms of faculty development. It is precisely in the area of academic affairs that the scholarship on historically black colleges and universities is rather thin.

In addition to the literature that deals with the enrollment trends of black students or that advocates, in usually very broad terms, a vital and continuing role for the historically black colleges and universities as such, research has been devoted primarily to student characteristics and performance, institutional finances and resources, and legal questions.[5] These are pressing issues indeed, but there are surprisingly few studies on the *academic* functioning of black colleges and universities. Those that have been published tend to be descriptions about faculty or a particular program at a single institution.[6]

The lack of systematically ordered, comparative studies about the academic responses made by public four-year black institutions to their new environments is serious. It makes it difficult for those directly involved in making decisions affecting black colleges and universities to inform themselves about what other historically black colleges and universities in similar situations are finding feasible and productive in the academic realm.

Any vision of the future of black colleges and universities will have to have a significant academic and curricular component if it is to guide advocacy and policy. Perhaps this is less problematic in the first of the three likely models that I outlined in this chapter, because the general-purpose regional state college represents a fairly clearly chartered path. Even in this case, however, there are specific questions about the region and student constituencies that need to be addressed in curricular terms if the institution is going to be successful in its new role.

The second model, that of an institution with specialized programs of whatever kind, requires careful curricular thinking about how specialized the institution should become, what kinds of curricula outside the areas of specialization would be necessary to support the central programs, and how the institution would sustain its focus on specialized programs in light of what other institutions have experienced in the way of strong pressures to become more all-purpose institutions.

The third model described here—a general, racially integrated state college with special emphases on serving black, Latino, and other minority students—raises the most interesting and complex curricular issues. It is disappointing to find them so seldom analyzed in the higher education literature. Should it be a conventional curriculum with special supports available to students who are not of mainstream white backgrounds? Is it a curriculum informed by the educational conceptions outlined in Chapter 7, on black studies? What are the other important models, and how do they fit the specific settings in which a historically black college or university finds itself?

These are crucial questions that need to be addressed, because their answers will affect the pattern of one of the most exciting and problematic transformations occurring in U.S. higher education. As noted earlier, this is a transformation that has important implications for the future of institutions that have in the past performed the function of providing access to groups disadvantaged in one way or another, a function vital to democratic education in the nation.

12

Excellence, Hierarchy, and Democratic Education

In speaking of the importance of widespread access for democratic education, I have noted, both in the Introduction and in Chapter 11, the need for that access to be to high-quality education. In several other chapters, I have discussed quality education at some length in terms of curriculum and pedagogy. As these chapters have shown, quality education is a multidimensional concept. In this chapter I address the relationship between quality undergraduate education and democracy in terms of institutional structures.

DEFINITIONS OF QUALITY

Instead of defining quality education in terms of the development of students' intellectual powers and desirable habits of mind—in curricular and pedagogical terms—quality education can be and often is defined in institutional terms—as that which occurs in a quality college. What is a quality college? In general use, there are three principal indicators of institutional quality: an outstanding reputation among those who count; generous amounts of educational resources; and highly selective admissions standards. All three indicators are inputs into the process, but they have no necessary relationship to the quality of educational result. Nonetheless, they offer criteria for the best, and the last two can establish a comprehensive scale of colleges and universities by quality. (See Kuh, 1981, and Lawrence & Green, 1980, for surveys of the literature on assessing quality and ratings.)

It is no secret that some institutions are considered to be better than others. Reisman (1956) presents a classical description of this hierarchy, which he describes as a snakelike academic procession in which institutions are arrayed from the best at the head and the worst at the tail. The Carnegie typology of institutions of higher education, listed in Appendix A, gives a rough approximation of this academic procession.[1]

There are at least two reasons for the increasing importance of a status hierarchy among colleges and universities in the twentieth century. As I argued in Chapter 1, one reason was the convergence of college and university curricula, led by the disciplinary major programs, in virtually every liberal arts college or division in the late nineteenth and early twentieth centuries. Increased curricular uniformity, especially in disciplinary majors, has flattened out much of the diversity of U.S. higher education and led to a standardization that has permitted more direct comparability among institutions. (For related interpretations, see Reisman 1956; Trow, 1984; and especially Geiger, 1986, who carefully shows how competition, growth, and organizational change have promoted such convergence among institutions.)

As I also discussed in Chapter 1, these internal, curricular changes combined with another, contemporaneous development occurring outside the academy: The creation of professional certification systems that depended on college degrees contributed to substantially greater numbers of people attending colleges and universities. This in turn meant that a college education, in and of itself, became less potent as a symbol of social status. In response, students and their families became interested in magnifying status differences among colleges and college degrees. This view is central to the study by Levine (1986), who begins with a quotation by Fussell (1982) that clearly expresses (and perhaps overstates) the argument:

> In the absence of a system of hereditary ranks and titles, without a tradition of honors conferred by a monarch, and with no well-known status ladder even of high-class regiments to confer various degrees of chachet, Americans have had to depend for their mechanism of snobbery far more than other peoples on their college and university hierarchy. [p. 25]

So, increasing curricular uniformity, permitting easier interinstitutional comparisons, and the status-seeking efforts by students and their families (aided and abetted by the institutions that served them) produced both the possibility and the incentive to differentiate colleges along a single dimension, called "quality," which has become the primary and often exclusive criterion for distinguishing among institutions. Competition among colleges and universities, including the efforts by upwardly mobile institutions to become "higher quality" through emulation, proceeds in uniform terms, promoting even greater conformity. As a consequence, institutional competition reifies and strengthens narrow conceptions of what constitutes quality—and thus quality education—among institutions.

QUALITY "VERSUS" DEMOCRATIC EDUCATION

The next step in the analysis is to look at the relationship between quality education, in the terms set by the hierarchical ordering of institutional quality, and democratic education, defined in terms of social structure and access to quality education. The best study of this relationship is by Astin (1985), who asserts the need for a "systems" rather than an "institutional" approach to these matters. Astin's skepticism about the significance of conventional measures of quality is informative and refreshing. Although commonly recognized, his demonstration of the extremely high correlation among the institutional rankings produced by the three measures of undergraduate institutional quality is striking. The institutions with the best reputations among, say, college presidents and other informed groups surveyed are also the institutions with the most selective admissions standards (student SAT scores, high school grades, and class standing). And as Table 12.1 shows, the institutions with the most selective admissions standards are also the institutions that utilize the most educational resources per student (physical plant, library holdings, faculty salaries, student:faculty ratios, and student services). This is a relationship that holds right on down through the entire range of selectivity. So reputation, selectivity, and resources—three common measures of institutional quality—yield very much the same rankings.

Per-student expenditures, therefore, are an adequate proxy for the combined indexes of institutional quality, and Table 12.1 shows that levels of per-student expenditures in 1,333 colleges and universities (over half of the total) equal about one-third the per-student expenditures of the top 81 institutions (3 percent of the total). While there is a break below these elite institutions, where the gradient of per-student expenditures becomes much less steep, the range is substantial. The point is that institutional quality, by these measures, is very unevenly distributed. The pattern is probably not unlike that of the distribution of income among families and individuals, although less unevenly distributed than wealth.

Turning now to the issue of democratic access to quality education, there is a very close and positive relationship between these

TABLE 12.1 Indicators of Institutional Hierarchy

Selectivity: Mean SAT for entering freshmen[a]	Number of Institutions	Parental Income of Freshmen		Per-Student Educational Expenditures
		% > $50,000	% < $15,000	
1300 or higher	14	47.1	6.8	$11,243
1225 - 1299	20	39.1	8.0	8,944
1150 - 1224	47	39.4	7.1	9,037
1075 - 1149	78	24.8	12.5	5,624
1000 - 1074	215	22.5	51.7	5,095
925 - 999	310	17.0	15.7	4,183
850 - 924	673	10.5	22.8	3,816
775 - 849	1,106	10.4	25.7	3,474
below 775	227	7.2	40.1	3,676
All Institutions	2,690	15.2	16.0	4,418

[a]ACT scores have been converted to SAT equivalents.

[b]Part-time students are counted as one-third, and graduate students are counted as three under-graduates; dollar amount includes expenditures for instruction, academic support, student services, administration, and physical plant, 1981-1982.

Source: Adapted from Alexander W. Astin, *Achieving Academic Excellence* (San Francisco: Jossey-Bass, 1985), pp. 6, 9.

measures of institutional quality and measures of material and cultural advantage in students' backgrounds (parents' income and levels of education). That is, students who attend the best colleges and universities are also the students whose parents have the highest incomes and the most education among all college students. As Table 12.1 suggests, the relationship between selectivity and family income again holds, virtually without an exception, right on down through the entire range of institutions arrayed by selectivity.

Astin (1985) handles these and a number of other pertinent relationships with characteristic clarity and insight, and he has no trouble in identifying the consequences of these arrangements for students from diverse class and ethnic backgrounds. The allocation of educational resources in U.S. colleges and universities strongly favors the institutions attended by ethnically mainstream undergraduate students from privileged backgrounds, and undergraduate students from less privileged backgrounds and with lower levels of academic achievement attend institutions with substantially fewer educational resources per student. Even though this is not as strong a conclusion as that by Hansen and Weisbrod (1969), who show that public higher education in California is a mechanism by which lower-income people subsidize the education of young people from affluent families, it is sufficient for our current purposes. (Also see Adams, 1977.)

Astin (1985) repeatedly emphasizes that hierarchical rankings of institutions are essentially subjective constructs, residing in the "psychological" realm. That is, the system of differential institutional quality is primarily sustained by a set of firmly held popular beliefs about those institutions, and these beliefs are the reason that top-ranked institutions are able to attract greater volumes of resources and better prepared students from prosperous homes. Clark (1987) implicitly agrees with this line of causation, although he stresses the positive aspects of hierarchy.

Emphasizing that educational resources follow institutional status obscures the way in which status *and* resources flow to institutions that serve the wealthy and powerful, who possess disproportionate amounts of status and resources in the broader society. It is not satisfactory to use institutional prestige as an independent and determining variable to explain, for instance, why black colleges and universities historically have operated with severe disadvantages in respect to academic resources and student preparedness. All three indicators of conventionally defined "quality" in higher education—selectivity, reputation, and resources—are determined by other factors; they are simply alternative measures of privilege.

In spite of what I see to be questionable attributions of causation, Astin (1982) certainly does demonstrate that, if poorer and especially minority students do go to college, it is likely that they will attend a college with far fewer resources per student than the colleges attended by students with material advantages. Astin's recognition of differential access to higher education institutions of differential status and quality puts his work in a very different league from the vast majority of studies. Most of these are written by academics in comfortable situations at or near the top of the status pyramid, and they seldom notice the existence of the pyramid, much less its significance.[2]

It is also important to look at the correspondence between certain kinds of students and certain kinds of colleges in directly pedagogical terms. For instance, one can reformulate the variability among colleges and universities in straightforward educational terms: Higher education resources are systematically and consistently distributed among U.S. colleges and universities in such a pattern that students are educated in institutions where levels of per-student educational resources are *inversely* related to their educational needs, as indicated by performance in high school and SAT examinations. An alternative formulation, from the faculty's perspective, is that the students easiest to teach are taught with relatively generous amounts of educational resources, while those most difficult to teach are taught with relatively few resources.

This strong correspondence is not just a matter of comparing per-student support at the extreme points on the institutional spectrum (e.g., community colleges compared to Ivy League universities). Table 12.1 shows that the relationship between educational resources and students' educational (and social) backgrounds holds very well throughout the entire range of student selectivity in both public and private colleges and universities.

Whatever role such a correlation between resources and client groups may play in the reproduction of social privilege and power, this same principle—spending more on the education of those who need it less—is also evident *within* institutions. It can be seen, for instance, by comparing the resources available in a particular university for teaching graduate students versus those for teaching under-graduates; indeed, many public systems have codified this disparity by weighting graduate student enrollments more heavily than under-graduate enrollments in formulae that generate the number of faculty positions appropriate for a given number of students. It also occurs within undergraduate programs; one need only compare average class sizes and per-student facilities for lower-division students to those for upper-division students (Study Group, 1984). In both cases, the results are analogous to those found among institutions, even though within institutions students' social-class backgrounds and initial academic readiness are not substantially different.

But, returning to the main argument, which is the relationships among institutions, higher education clearly is not the only semipublic service distributed in this manner. Primary and secondary education, medical services, and public libraries are other examples (e.g., Weaver & Weaver, 1979). I believe, however, that the distributional phenomenon is more frequently recognized in debates about these other services and activities and that the pattern may not be so consistent. In higher education, the strong and negative relationship between the availability of educational resources and students' needs (and the difficulty of teaching them) is so pervasive and consistent that it deserves being known as the "Iron Law of Higher Education Resource Allocation." While the discovery of such a law cannot but be some-what heartening for a social scientist, who seldom finds such powerful regularities in social relationships, it is abundantly clear that the current situation falls short of the equal-access standard of democratic education.

Unlike the relationship between educational quality and democratic education as defined in curricular and pedagogical terms, the relationship between quality education and democratic education defined in terms of institutions and social structure is not harmonious. To the extent that quality institutions are identified by enrolling well-prepared and affluent students, and institutions' resource advantage depends on this enrollment pattern, the structural conception of quality and democratic education leads to a profound pessimism about the prospects, and perhaps even desirability, of democratic education in access terms. There are only so many colleges and universities that will be able to be quality institutions in these standard terms. Increasing democratic access would thus, by definition, lead to a dilution of educational quality, either by changing enrollment compositions in the best colleges and universities or by diverting resources away from them in order to increase the flow toward middle- and lower-ranking institutions. This conclusion, as often as it is voiced, is an artifact of inadequate definitions of quality.

CUTTING ACROSS DEFINITIONS OF QUALITY

The number of recent proposals for improving undergraduate education is large and increasing, and they are highly diverse in content. Nostalgia for a fictitious past is a theme common to many, but an even more striking similarity is in what they consistently avoid mentioning. One does not have to be involved with deconstructionist approaches to textual criticism in order to recognize the significance of consistent omissions; the silence on the strongly hierarchical nature of institutional quality and the undemocratic nature of access is practically deafening. This is for good reason: The bulk of scholarship on higher education, including the special reports that receive a wide hearing, is produced precisely by those who benefit directly from current structures. This is not to impugn the integrity of those writing the studies and reports; I am not talking about bad faith or deliberately self-serving manipulation of topics and data. Nevertheless, it is not surprising to find that an advantaged group of people do consistently see those structures (when they actually do see them) as reasonable, equitable, and serving the interests of all. As in other dimensions of inequality, a form of trickle-down approach is popular in higher education (e.g., Clark, 1987).

In order to address systematically the relationship between quality education and democratic education, we need to integrate the dual definitions of quality that have been listed: (1) curriculum and pedagogy and (2) reputation, selectivity in admissions, and resources. What is needed is a conception of quality that encompasses both of these standard approaches so that they can be incorporated into a unified analytical framework.

This takes us back to Astin (1985), whose central argument is that what makes a college a good college (and an education a quality education) is its ability to change students in tangible and desirable ways. By this criterion, standard indicators of institutional quality miss the point. Reputation is suspect as a measure in any case; resources are the inputs of the process; curriculum and pedagogy are how those inputs are organized as educational vehicles; and the ability of admitted students is the beginning point of the process—the raw material, if you will. None of these measures of institutional and educational quality is an indicator of the achievement of change.

While levels of educational outcomes are more reasonable measures, they still are not, by themselves, good measures. When a college recruits bright, academically well prepared, ambitious students from comfortable homes, it is likely that, upon graduation, those students will score well on exit examinations (just as they did on entrance examinations) and subsequently do quite well in their postcollege professional careers. This does not mean that the college has contributed much to those students' successes. "Good" colleges and universities may simply be screening students for highly paid occupations and prestigious roles, leaving students relatively unaffected except for changes attributable to four years of maturation.

On the other hand, an education that goes on in a less prestigious college may significantly enhance students' skills and cognitive abilities and transform their sensibilities, but the level of educational outcome will not be a sufficient indicator of this occurrence. Outcomes are too closely tied to where students started to be a measure of what the college or university contributed. Astin (1985) calls the (desirable) changes in students attributable to college education "talent development," but I prefer to use the more common term, "value added," borrowed from economics and national income accounting.

The value-added approach has important implications for the debate about whether higher education's contributions to class reproduction and social mobility are primarily a matter of screening or of educating. (See G. Williams, 1984, for a good discussion of this debate.) "Low value added" suggests primacy of the screening function. As noted earlier, screening is the process by which winners are selected rather than created, and by which others are culled for lower and intermediate positions in the occupational hierarchy by being relegated to institutions at the lower or intermediate levels in the institutional hierarchy. In contrast, "high value added" means that college education contributes to students' capabilities and thus their ability to move upward, relative to their parents' positions, in the social structure. Using a value-added analysis makes it possible to disaggregate the debate, which does not sufficiently acknowledge the stratification of higher education and the implications of that stratification for questions of screening versus educating.

Closely related to the screening-versus-educating question are two examples of thinking along value-added lines. The first one concerns the competitive urge of institutions to admit the "best" students. Klitgaard (1985) considers this a natural and desirable aspiration, and, from the vantage point of Harvard University's admissions office, he discusses such efforts in terms of "choosing elites." To Astin (1985), however, using the value-added approach to education and thinking of higher education as a system serving the nation, this form of competition seems wasteful and beside the main point.

If the goal of the education system is to raise national educational levels as much as is feasible within the constraints of resources and organization, institutions ought to seek to admit those students whom a college education will benefit the most—those students for whom the institution could add the greatest educational value, irrespective of where they are beginning. This conclusion is more interesting than and very different from what the logic of conventional premises indicates, but it might lead to an admissions policy likely to be resisted by an institution's faculty, who enjoy teaching better-prepared students.

Moreover, the same institution's admissions officer is no doubt conscious that institutional "quality" (or the illusion of quality), defined in part by the achievement levels of its incoming classes, is one of the most (if not the most) important reasons that students will choose to come to that college. As such, the admissions officer will be justifiably worried about the risks of trying to sell the institution to prospective students and their parents on the grounds that it is an excellent place for, say, mediocre students whose educational levels will be vastly improved.

A second example of the insight that can be gained by value-added analysis emerges in the area of values changes in students. Even though a college education may make students a bit more tolerant of diversity and a bit more politically liberal, there is little likelihood that college will wreak profound changes in a student's values. Despite a large amount of writing about values education (e.g., Morrill, 1980), colleges seem to have only marginal effects on students' core values. For instance, if colleges and universities *significantly* affected students' values, one would expect that good numbers of well-educated youth would be willing to move downward in the social order. The idea of downward mobility may seem capricious, but it should be considered an important indicator of changes in attitudes and convictions wrought by college and university experience, even though it is ignored by many of those who specialize in values education.

Students entering colleges and universities in the 1980s have been strongly registering material success as the preeminent purpose of going to college. If students' values and thinking were really transformed by a college education, one would expect to find a good number of students from privileged family backgrounds committing themselves to public school teaching, museum curatorships, nursing, social work, and other occupations with significant rewards but yielding considerably less income and status than that garnered by their parents. This would mean, once again, that their college education was a vehicle of downward mobility.

While this would be the most dramatic expression of such a transformation, similar changes should also be evident among those students from farther down the social pyramid and attending lower-status institutions. Does a college education, by helping these students to develop alternative aspirations, blunt some of their eagerness for material acquisition and for getting ahead, or does it simply enhance their ability to succeed in terms of the same values and ambitions they possessed when they arrived on campus?

Of course, looking again at the admissions office, there is a problem of reportage. If significant value transformations of the kind I have described were to occur with some frequency among a particular college's students, it is unlikely that the college would be very enthusiastic about advertising these to prospective students and their parents, who in their untransformed states would not be attracted to such an institution.

Even if we drop the values side of education's effects and stick to a narrower sense of value added that stresses the development of skills and cognition, it is difficult to measure it accurately and reliably. Astin's (1985) discussions of the problems involved in measuring value added are interesting and suggestive regarding the principles and desirable qualities of assessment, but they are not very precise (see also "Assessment Update," 1987; Astin, 1990). Nonetheless, Astin's (1985) point stands: The value-added conception is much more appropriate for assessing the effectiveness of educational institutions, and it is where assessment efforts should focus. While the development and testing of instruments for measuring value added are difficult, the idea of measuring it is theoretically no more difficult than measuring performance at any particular area or level. Value added measures simply require before and after components.

Defining educational quality by the changes achieved in students' skills, knowledge, and various capacities leads to useful and provocative perspectives on institutional quality. For example, there is a definite possibility that comparative measures of value added would reveal that the education of undergraduates completing their studies in many regional state colleges contains more value added than the education of those graduating from Ivy League universities. The same statistics may very well also confirm that the absolute levels of achievement in the former is lower than those of the latter. Nevertheless, the demonstration that regional state colleges actually do more educating than Ivy League universities would be an interesting finding, and one that would subvert a number of firmly held assumptions about the relative caliber of various higher education institutions.

Although this example is not improbable, it does represent a limiting case, and we ought to look at a less extreme one. Although value-added measures might determine that Ivy League universities rather than regional state colleges are conferring more educational value, there is a good chance that the differences between them in value added would turn out to be less than their differences in per-student expenditures. This weaker finding could be combined with certain plausible assumptions, such as that increases in educational resources will have about the same amount of educational effect that already employed resources have (i.e., that marginal changes are roughly equal to averages). The result would still suggest that a greater contribution to national educational levels would be made by directing educational resources to regional state colleges and universities (and perhaps to community colleges), rather than to elite institutions.

This is a different conclusion from what emerges from using standard criteria of quality, from which it is easy to conclude that the putatively best institutions provide the best education (and perhaps are the only institutions in which real learning is taking place). Through regarding quality in this way, elite institutions appear to be the models to which all higher education should aspire in order to raise national levels of educational quality. As noted earlier, increasing democratic access invariably leads to lowered quality, according to these convictions.

By redefining educational quality along value-added lines, however, not only is there likely to be some salutary diminution of the snobbery contained in current rankings of excellence, but, more important, we will be able to see that the relationship between excellence and access is not a matter of trading off one for the other. Excellent education in value-added terms requires the curricular and pedagogical reforms associated with educational quality and democratic education, augmented educational resources, and *increased access to higher education.*

Joining the value-added conception of educational excellence to an appreciation for the extent to which higher education is a hierarchical system serving differentiated clienteles would reorient and broaden the debate about the public policy directions most appropriate for improving national educational levels. This debate could not avoid explicitly addressing the distinction between absolute levels of achievement and value added in the various tiers of the system, and thus the relationships among the performance of the different segments of the higher education system, group privilege, individual mobility, and democratic values.

As a consequence, the obstacles to achieving substantial increases in educational quality and democratic education in the higher education system could no longer be misconstrued, and misconstrued in a way that works to the advantage of those with the most advantages. Instead of being faced with supposedly ineluctable choices between educational excellence and access, the obstacles would clearly and accurately be seen as matters of social power that need to be addressed by political means.

This situation stands in sharp contrast to my argument on curricular reform, which maintained that significant and positive innovations in curriculum and pedagogy do not require sweeping changes. The changes needed to improve educational quality in the realms of social structure and democratic access are most definitely not modest.

APPENDIXES

NOTES

REFERENCES

INDEX

ABOUT THE AUTHOR

APPENDIX A

The Carnegie Foundation's Classification of Institutions of Higher Education

The Carnegie Council on Policy Studies in Higher Education first published its institutional classification in 1973 and revised it in 1976. The most recent edition has been issued by the Carnegie Foundation for the Advancement of Teaching, as *A Classification of Institutions of Higher Education, 1987 Edition.* I have used a slightly consolidated version of their categories, combining Research Universities I and Research Universities II into a single category and Doctoral-Granting Universities I and Doctoral-Granting Universities II into a single category as well. Although the chapters in this book emphasize undergraduate education in institutions that grant at least the baccalaureate degree, I have included the two-year institutions and specialized institutions in the definitions and in Table A.1, in order to maintain a sense of proportion about the entire sector of U.S. higher education.

In his foreword to the Carnegie Foundation (1987a) book on institutional classification, Ernest Boyer writes,

> This classification of colleges and universities is *not* intended to establish a hierarchy among higher learning institutions. Rather, the aim is to group institutions according to their shared characteristics, and we oppose the use of the classifications as a way to make qualitative distinctions among the separate sectors. We have in this country a rich variety of institutions that serves a variety of needs. We celebrate this diversity, acknowledging that our system of higher education is the envy of the world. [p. 2]

Readers will recall that, in Chapter 12, I explore one of the dimensions of this institutional diversity—the remarkable way in which that diversity expresses differential privilege among groups of people.

Turning to the categories themselves, the Carnegie Foundation's (1987a) most recent criteria for placing colleges and universities in the

TABLE A.1. Higher Education Institutions Arranged by the Carnegie Classification

	Institutions			Enrollment		
	Number	%	%Public	Total	%	%Public
Research Universities	104	3.1	68.3	2,209,000	17.9	81.4
Doctoral-Granting Univ.	109	3.2	57.8	1,220,000	9.9	70.2
Comprehensive C. & U. 1	424	12.5	67.0	2,971,000	24.2	76.7
Comprehensive C. & U. 2	171	5.0	27.5	332,000	2.7	29.2
Liberal Arts Colleges 1	142	4.2	1.4	214,000	1.7	2.3
Liberal Arts Colleges 2	430	12.7	7.0	370,000	3.0	10.5
Two-Year Institutions	1,367	40.3	72.1	4,518,000	36.7	94.1
Specialized Institutions	642	18.9	10.3	467,000	3.8	28.1
TOTAL	3,389	100.0	45.7	12,301,000	100.0	76.9

Source: Carnegie Foundation for the Advancement of Teaching, *A Classification of Institutions of Higher Education,* 1987 Edition (Princeton, NJ: Author, 1987), p. 5.

categories are as follows. It should be noted, however, that they seem in several cases to be substantially different from the criteria for the same categories in the 1976 edition.

Research Universities (RU): These institutions offer a full range of baccalaureate programs, are committed to graduate education through the doctorate degree, and give high priority to research. They receive annually at least $12.5 million in federal support for research and development and award at least 50 Ph.D. degrees each year.

Doctorate-Granting Universities (DG): In addition to offering a full range of baccalaureate programs, the mission of these institutions includes a commitment to graduate education through the doctorate degree. They award annually 20 or more Ph.D. degrees in three or more disciplines.

Comprehensive Universities and Colleges I (CUC 1): These institutions offer baccalaureate programs and, with few exceptions, graduate education through the master's degree. More than half of their baccalaureate degrees are awarded in two or more occupational or professional disciplines, such as engineering or business administration. All of the institutions in this group enroll at least 2,500 students.

Comprehensive Universities and Colleges II (CUC 2): These institutions award more than half of their baccalaureate degrees in two or more occupational or professional disciplines, such as engineering or business administration, and many also offer graduate education through the masters degree. All of the colleges and universities in this group enroll between 1,500 and 2,500 students.

Liberal Arts Colleges I (LA 1): These highly selective institutions are primarily undergraduate colleges that award more than half of their baccalaureate degrees in arts and science fields.

Liberal Arts Colleges II (LA 2): These institutions are primarily undergraduate colleges that are less selective and award more than half of their degrees in liberal arts fields. This category also includes a group of colleges (identified with an asterisk in the volume's actual listings) that award less than half their degrees in liberal arts fields, but, with fewer than 1,500 students, are too small to be considered comprehensive.

Two-Year Community, Junior, and Technical Colleges: These institutions offer certificate or degree programs through the Associate of Arts level and, with few exceptions, offer no baccalaureate degrees.

Professional Schools and Other Specialized Institutions: These institutions offer degrees ranging from the bachelor's to the doctorate. At least 50 percent of the degrees awarded by these institutions are in a single specialized field.

APPENDIX B

Cost Savings Due to Inflation-Induced Price Changes During the 1970s

In order to illustrate the magnitude of the net budgetary savings derived from the uneven changes in prices during the inflation of the 1970s, Table B.1 uses data from Table 2.1 to portray some hypothetical budgetary figures for an important subset of higher education institutions—privately controlled 4-year colleges.

The table is constructed to compare what costs would have been in 1980 if the private colleges had purchased exactly the same quantities of goods and services (including labor) as they had in 1973. The critical comparison, though, is not between 1973 and 1980 costs, but between 1980 costs under two different price conditions: increases at the rate of the overall economy (CPI), and increases at the actual rates given in Table 2.1. The difference between these amounts is the net budgetary gain, or "inflation dividend," that accrued to colleges over this period.

The source of these cost savings was the divergent rates of change among prices paid by colleges and universities, divergences made possible by inflation. The figures in the "1980 CPI" column, in which there are no *relative* changes, are comparable to a situation in which there were no changes in any prices at all. Relative price changes did occur, however, as shown in the figures in the "1980 Actual" column, and the result was a financial windfall for college and university budgets. The role of inflation in this process was critical.

The inflation dividend figures shown in the table may be considerably underestimated because of the following:

1. The assumption of identical quantities purchased, needed to make the figures comparable, probably overestimates the amounts in the "1980 Actual" column because institutions did adjust the composition of their purchases away from goods and services with the most rapidly rising prices.

TABLE B. 1 Hypothetical Aggregate Budget for Private 4-Year Colleges ($millions)

Budget Category	1973	1980 CPI[a]	Actual[b]	Inflation Dividend
Professional salaries	$2,743.1	$4,976.0	$4,004.9	$971.1
Nonprofessional salaries and wages	$709.4	$1,286.9	$1,195.3	$91.6
Fringe benefits	$425.6	$772.0	$881.4	-$109.4
Contracted Services,				
Supplies, Equipment	$851.3	$1,544.3	$1,688.1	-$143.8
TOTAL OPERATING BUDGETS	$4,729.4	$8,579.2	$7,769.8	$809.5

[a]Costs for identical goods and services adjusted for inflation at the same rate as the Consumer Price Index (CPI), 181.4%

[b]Costs for identical goods and services adjusted for inflation according to differential increases shown in Table 2.1.

Source: The 1973 actual operating budget figures are from Paul F. Martins and Norman J. Brandt, *Financial Statistics of Institutions of Higher Education: Current Funds Revenues and Expenditures, 1972-1973* (Washington, DC: Government Printing Office, 1976), p. 15.

2. The amounts listed for "fringe benefits" are probably exaggerated, and some of these costs (e.g., tuition remission for faculty children) are not out-of-pocket expenses.
3. It is likely that the relative importance of contracted services, supplies, and equipment for private colleges, which generally have smaller campuses than public colleges and universities, is less than the all-institution average used here.
4. It is likely that faculty salary changes in private colleges lagged behind the all-institution average (Hansen, 1980).

Underestimated or not, the total inflation dividend calculated in Table B.1 is a substantial sum. College budgets, of course, experienced real growth in addition to inflation in the 1973–1980 period; the aggregate budget for private 4-year colleges was in fact $9,576.3 million (N. Brandt, personal communication). Even so, the $809.3 million "inflation dividend" represents a savings of 8.5% of the actual budget. Another way to get a sense of proportion about the size of the inflation dividend is to recognize that it would have paid the salaries of 43,567 faculty members at the average faculty salary prevailing in independent 4-year colleges during fiscal year 1980 (Hansen, 1980).

It is interesting to note what portion of the inflation dividend is directly attributable to the real decline in faculty salaries of the period: Over two-thirds of the savings in personnel salaries came from faculty, and indeed, nearly three-quarters of the total savings due to inflation came at their expense.

Notes

Chapter 1

1. In addition to the works cited in the text, see Geiger (1986), Hawkins, (1979), Higham (1979), Jencks and Reisman (1968), Kevles (1979), Metzger (1987), Ross (1979), and Veysey (1965, 1979) for excellent treatments of organization and intellectual changes in late nineteenth and early twentieth century colleges and universities.

2. Most of the works cited earlier refer to an undifferentiated "academic profession." For other examples of this, see Wilensky (1970) and Metzger (1977). Light (1974) and Weaver (1981) make clear statements about the character of academic disciplines in colleges and universities. Additional useful discussions on disciplines and departments are presented by Clark (1987), Dressel and Reichard (1970), Straus (1973), and Smith (1983), and in the concise expression of different points of view in the collection of essays by McHenry (1977).

3. It is always dubious to speak of "institutions" as though their existence were independent from those working in them. Veysey (1965) presents an excellent discussion of how the idea of the impersonal, even transcendent, college and university became prominent in the early twentieth century.

Chapter 2

1. Bowen (1980) is a clear and intelligent study of higher education costs and the issues surrounding them. In spite of the book's impressive scope, however, it does not deal with the specific subject of this chapter, and neither it nor this chapter considers the cost implications of increasing faculty work loads. Navin and Magura (1977) explain how to construct cost indexes for individual colleges and universities, and O'Keefe (1987) gives an interesting review of changes in costs at six colleges and universities over the last few years.

2. Bowen (1980) and Baldridge et al. (1978) provide good discussions of college and university goals. As noted earlier, Bowen (1980) proposes the "revenue theory of costs" for higher education and demonstrates and interprets the post-1970 decline in direct educational costs per student. Also see the

National Center (1980b) for an examination of tuition and room and board charges.

Chapter 3

1. For instance, consider Abraham Flexner's address to the National Conference on Social Welfare in 1915, in which he is pessimistic about social work ever becoming a real profession (for *women*), and compare it to the functionalist classic by Davis and Moore (1945).

Chapter 4

1. Aarons (1985), Bell (1966), Brann (1979), Churchill (1983), Dressel and Marcus (1982), Gamson (1984), Kavaloski (1979), Kurfiss (1988), Lee (1967), McCauley (1982), McPeck (1981), Mitroff (1982), Patterson and Longsworth (1966), Project on Redefining (1985), Shor (1980), Smith (1983), Weber (1983), and Wegener (1978) all promote the inquiry idea, whether or not they call it by that name, and they indicate the wide range of perspectives from which it can be implemented. Kurfiss (1988) provides a good survey of the variety of meanings contained in this general approach to teaching.

2. Kurfiss (1988), McPeck (1981), and Walters (1986) criticize these tendencies in the critical-thinking movement; see the examples (and especially the textbooks) that they cite, as well as Brookfield (1987) and Woditsch, Schlesinger, and Giardina (1987) for recent examples that threaten to reduce critical thinking to a technique.

Another variant of educational thinking closely related to what I call critical inquiry is Perry's (1981) frequently cited application of Piaget's developmental hierarchies of thinking to learning in colleges and universities. Garver (1986) and Kurfiss (1988) offer useful reviews and thoughtful criticisms of some of the implications of applying Piagetian concepts in this manner. Katz and Henry (1988) provide perhaps the best example of this approach, focusing their work solidly on the content of what is to be taught.

3. This position clearly is in direct opposition to that espoused by Phenix (1962), who argues that "the structure of things is revealed, not invented, . . . *given*, not chosen, and if man is to gain insight he must employ the right concepts and methods. . . . [Therefore,] disciplines are the only proper source of the curriculum" (p. 280).

4. Tierney (1989), in an excellent study, uses an expanded concept of process that includes the ethos and culture of institutions as they operate and make decisions, in order to discuss democratic education.

5. Hampshire College insists that student work in the concentration (structurally equivalent to the major) be cumulative and coherent, but this is possible only because of Hampshire's peculiar and demanding examination system, which operates outside the course system. See Weaver (1989) for a description and discussion of the system.

Chapter 5

1. Empire State College, with branches throughout New York State; the Metropolitan State College in Minneapolis; and the University Without Walls at the University of Massachusetts, Amherst are all unconventional schools that do not have campuses and whose principal clientele is older students. They all recognize the vital importance of the type of advising I am advocating and have structured it into their curricula in different ways.

Chapter 6

1. Zeichner (1983) provides a compact description of "behavioristic teacher education," which he considers the predominant mode in teacher education programs. By its positivism, such education constitutes training, as I have defined it. The same article is also very good on inquiry approaches.

Chapter 8

1. There also has been surprisingly little discussion of statistics teaching, even of the instrumental type. In spite of the increasingly quantitative character of the social sciences, articles on statistics teaching are extremely scarce in social science teaching journals. Even the *Journal of Economic Education* and *Teaching of Psychology* have been virtually silent on this area of study so vital to the discipline. See Table 10.5, which shows the infrequency of such articles in five social science teaching journals.

2. One indication of the lack of attention to descriptive statistics in introductory statistics courses in the minimal space devoted to such material in the 43 introductory statistics textbooks I have surveyed. Twenty-six of these books were designed for the social and behavioral sciences in general; the remaining 17 were written for statistics courses in economics, sociology, psychology, political science, or history. Descriptive statistics constituted less than 10 percent of the total text pages of 19 of these books, between 10 and 20 percent in another 14, and more than 25 percent in only 2. (The list of the 43 textbooks consulted is available from me on request.) In addition to these textbooks, Huff (1954) and Zeisel (1968) offer two short, useful books on descriptive statistics aimed at general audiences. Huff is especially delightful and in spite of its age is still excellent for students with "statistics anxiety." It has achieved the deserved status of a classic.

3. For sources of statistics appropriate for introductory courses oriented toward any discipline or specialization, see the index by Wasserman and Bernero (1977), which is extensive (976 pages), informative, and easily used. The U.S. Congressional Information Service publishes two comprehensive annual indexes: *American Statistical Index* and *Statistical Reference Index*. The first is for U.S. government statistical sources and the latter for other

statistical sources. Students will probably need a reference librarian's help in using either of these complex indexes.

Chapter 9

1. As discussed in Chapters 1 and 2, this has not always been the case. The set curricula and pedagogies of eighteenth- and early nineteenth-century colleges did not require an intellectually trained or gifted faculty. Handlin and Handlin (1970) and Kolesnik (1958) provide good analyses of the role of the faculty in earlier colleges.

2. In his review of the research on the relationship between faculty scholarship (disciplinary research) and teaching effectiveness, Finkelstein (1984) concludes that the correlation between the two is positive although small; however, when publication—rather than, say, time spent at research—is used to measure scholarship, the relationship becomes stronger.

3. Ways in which this integration can be accomplished were discussed at several sessions of the January 1987 meeting of the American Association of Colleges.

Chapter 10

1. Kuhn (1962) discusses the implications of "normal science" for its unquestioning acceptance of the tenets that dominate a discipline or field. The first and third chapters in this volume also discuss the nature of academic disciplines and their substantive definitions. Along these lines, it is notable that the *Journal of Economic Education* has recently broadened its editorial policy. It previously had declared that it wanted only articles based on "research" (i.e., pedagogical evaluation), thus severely limiting the journal's scope. Now its call for articles explicitly includes questions of *what* is to be taught.

Chapter 11

1. I discussed some of the vicissitudes of postintegration enrollment of black Americans in higher education at the beginning of Chapter 8. Its patterns have been studied extensively over the last few years by researchers such as Weinberg (1977), who places black student participation in higher education in the historical perspective of minority education in general. Other good empirical and interpretive studies include Astin (1982), Carnegie Foundation (1987), Hill (1983), Kingston (1984), Morris (1981), and National Center (1985). S. T. Hill (1981) and Webster (1981) deal specifically with the way black colleges have been affected by black students' enrolling in previously all-white college, and Bellamy (1983), C. I. Brown (1980), Buffkins (1977), Elam (1978), Libarkin (1984), and Standley (1978) address various issues around white students' enrolling in historically black schools.

2. The University of Mississippi Medical Center in Jackson, founded in

1955, has about 600 upper-division undergraduate students, mostly in nursing and medical technology, and black students constitute only a very small minority (about 7 percent) of the center's enrollment. Because of its proximity to Jackson State University, the center probably should be included in Table 11.3, but I have omitted it because of its specialized programs.

3. Molnar (1980) offers some insights on agricultural programs, and Ayres (1983) and Ivie (1982) discuss their reservations about emphasizing teacher education.

4. A large amount of the literature on historically black colleges and universities is devoted to arguments for this mission. Bullock (1967), Drake (1971), Fleming (1984), Lincoln (1971), Thompson (1984), and Tollett (1982) stress different aspects and are among the best of this advocacy literature. Jencks and Riesman (1968) and Thorpe (1975), for different reasons, have doubts about the prospects of historically black colleges and universities succeeding as primarily black institutions.

5. Allen (1987), Anthony (1981), Fleming (1984), and Powell (1981) are examples of researchers who focus on students; Bowles and DeCosta (1971), Elton (1974), and Sorkin (1969) compare institutional resources; and Baxter (1982) and Preer (1982) discuss the law and the litigation affecting historically black public colleges and universities. The evaluation of the Ford Foundation's Private Black College Program turned into a large-scale, inclusive research project on all black colleges and universities. Its design, however, conforms to the usual pattern, in that there appears to be little specific concern with directly academic matters. Also, it only briefly deals with historically black public colleges and universities. The project has been in process for years, and there seem to be no plans to publish it as a whole. Tollett (1982) is the author of one of the essays that was written under the project's auspices.

6. Lyson (1983), Miller (1981), and Uhl (1978) present a more academic orientation than most, while the work of Bracy (1977), Blake (1971), and Blake's Institute for Services to Education show the need for more attention to this sphere. Billingsley (1982) cogently argues the need for special efforts in faculty development. Mommsen (1973) and Morris (1972) are examples of the widespread concern about able black faculty being recruited away from black institutions (the "brain drain").

Another subset of the published literature relating to faculty at historically black colleges and universities is about white faculty. Davis (1979) and Warnat (1976) study white faculty at black institutions, and the works of Jabs (1973), Jones (1973), and Stringer (1974) are examples of a common genre: white professors writing about their experiences teaching, usually for a short period, at black colleges.

Chapter 12

1. Levy (1986) provides an excellent study of the development of hierarchies among Latin American universities. The different patterns of this phe-

nomenon in Latin America reveal interesting comparative perspectives on the process in the United States.

2. As an example, Clark (1987) productively incorporates the hierarchical status of colleges and universities into the center of his analyses. In doing so, however, he never notes that this hierarchy has any basis other than a "functional" division of labor, presumably staffed and enrolled according to meritocratic principles. He carefully avoids mentioning that the institutional hierarchy corresponds to patterns of inequality in the broader society. The consequently sanitized quality of the analysis reduces the impact of what should be a very influential book.

References

Aarons, A. B. (1985). Critical Thinking and the Baccalaureate Curriculum. *Liberal Education, 71*(2), 141–157.

Ackerman, J. B. (1973). The Arts in Higher Education. In C. Kaysen (Ed.), *Content and Context: Essays on College Education* (pp. 219–266). New York: McGraw-Hill.

Adams, W. (1977, May). Financing Public Higher Education. *American Economic Review, Papers and Proceedings*, pp. 86–89.

Adler, M. (1984). *The Paideia Program.* New York: Macmillan.

Allen, W. R. (1987). Black Colleges vs. White Colleges: The Fork in the Road for Black Students. *Change, 19*(3), 28–34.

Anthony, N. R. (1981). Ability/Aptitude, Personal, and Social Characteristics of Black College Students. *Journal of Negro Education, 50*(3), 346–353.

Arbeiter, S. (1987). Black Enrollments: The Case of the Missing Students. *Change, 19*(3), 14–19.

Aries, P. (1962). *Centuries of Childhood.* New York: Vintage Books.

Assessment Update. (1987). *AAHE Bulletin, 40*(4), 3–8.

Astin, A. W. (1982). *Minorities in American Higher Education: Recent Trends, Current Prospects, and Recommendations.* San Francisco: Jossey-Bass.

Astin, A. W. (1985). *Achieving Educational Excellence.* San Francisco: Jossey-Bass.

Astin, A. W. (1990). *Assessment for Excellence: The Philosophy and Practice of Assessment and Evaluation in Higher Education.* New York: Macmillan.

Austin, A. E., & Gamson, Z. F. (1983). *Academic Workplace: New Demands, Heightened Tensions* (ASHE-ERIC Higher Education Report No. 10). Washington, DC: Association for the Study of Higher Education.

Ayres, Q. W. (1983). Student Achievement at Predominantly White and Predominantly Black Universities. *American Education Research Journal, 20*(2), 291–304.

Baldridge, J. V., Curtis, D. V., Ecker, G., & Riley, G. L. (1978). *Policy Making and Effective Leadership.* San Francisco: Jossey-Bass.

Baldridge, J. V., Demerer, F. R., & Green, K. C. (1982). *The Enrollment Crisis: Factors, Actors, and Impacts* (AAHE-ERIC Higher Education Research Report No. 3). Washington, DC: American Association for Higher Education.

Baumol, W. J. (1967). The Macroeconomics of Unbalanced Growth. *American Economic Review, 57*, 415–426.

Baxter, F. V. (1982). The Affirmative Duty to Desegregate Institutions of Higher Education: Defining the Role of the Traditionally Black College. *Journal of Law and Education, 11*(1), 1–40.

Becher, T. (1984). The Cultural View. In B. R. Clark (Ed.), *Perspectives on Higher Education: Eight Disciplinary and Comparative Views* (pp. 165–198). Berkeley, CA: University of California Press.

Becher, T. (1987). The Disciplinary Shaping of the Profession. In B. P. Clark (Ed.), *The Academic Profession: National, Disciplinary, and Institutional Settings* (pp. 271–303). Berkeley, CA: University of California.

Bell, D. (1966). *The Reforming of General Education.* New York: Columbia University Press.

Bellamy, D. D. (1983). White Students—Historically Black Fort Valley State College: A Study of Reverse Desegregation in Georgia. *Negro Educational Review, 33*(3–4), 112–134.

Bennett, W. J. (1984, November 28). To Reclaim a Legacy: Text of Report on Humanities in Education. *Chronicle of Higher Education,* pp. 16–21.

Berrian, A. H. (1982). A New Order for Black Colleges. *AGB Reports, 24*(3), 35–38.

Bestor, A. E. (1953). *Educational Wastelands: The Retreat from Learning in Our Public Schools.* Urbana: University of Illinois Press.

Billingsley, A. (1982). Building Strong Faculties in Black Colleges. *Journal of Negro Education, 51*(1), 4–15.

Blake, E. (1971). Future Leadership Roles for Predominantly Black Colleges and Universities in American Higher Education. *Daedalus, 100*(3), 745–771.

Blau, P. M. (1973). *The Organization of Academic Work.* New York: John Wiley.

Bledstein, B. J. (1976) *The Culture of Professionalism: The Middle Class and the Development of Higher Education.* New York: W. W. Norton.

Bloom, A. (1987). *The Closing of the American Mind: How Higher Education Has Failed Democracy and Impoverished the Souls of Today's Students.* New York: Simon & Schuster.

Bowen, H. R. (1980). *The Costs of Higher Education: How Much Do Colleges and Universities Spend and How Much Should They Spend?* San Francisco: Jossey-Bass.

Bowen, H. R., & Schuster, J. H. (1986). *American Professors: A National Resource Imperiled.* New York: Oxford University Press.

Bowles, F., & DeCosta, F. A. (1971). *Between Two Worlds: A Profile of Negro Higher Education.* New York: McGraw-Hill.

Bowles, S., & Gintis, H. (1976). *Schooling in Capitalist America.* New York: Basic Books.

Boyer, E. L. (1987). *College: The Undergraduate Experience in America.* New York: Harper & Row.

Bracy, R. (1977). Interdependence: A Rationale for Restructuring Curricular Experiences in Black Higher Educational Institutions. *Negro Educational Review, 28,*(2), 100–106.

Brann, E. T. H. (1979). *Paradoxes of Education in a Republic.* Chicago: University of Chicago Press.

Breneman, D. W. (1981). Higher Education and the Economy. *Educational Record, 62*(2), 18–21.

Broido, J. (1979). Interdisciplinarity, Reflections on Methodology. In J. J. Kockelmans (Ed.), *Interdisciplinarity and Higher Education* (pp. 244–305). University Park: Pennsylvania State University Press.

Brookfield, S. D. (1987). *Developing Critical Thinkers: Challenging Adults to Explore Alternative Ways of Thinking and Acting.* San Francisco: Jossey-Bass.

Brown, C. I. (Ed.). (1980). *The White Student on the Black Campus: An Anthology of Essays and Studies* (Monograph No. 80-1). Durham: North Carolina Central University Institute of Desegregation.

Brown, C. I. (1983). *The White Student Enrolled at the Traditionally Black College and University.* Atlanta: Institute for Higher Educational Opportunity.

Brown, T. (1983, October–December). Black College Day in Historical Perspective. *Tony Brown's Journal,* pp. 4–8.

Buffkins, A. (1977). White Students at Black Schools. *Journal of Afro-American Issues, 5*(1), 66–71.

Bullock, H. A. (1967). *A History of Negro Education in the South, from 1619 to the Present.* Cambridge, MA: Harvard University Press.

Cadwallader, M. L. (1983). Reflections on Academic Freedom and Tenure. *Liberal Education, 69*(1), 1–170.

Cahn, S. M. (1986). *Saints and Scamps: Ethics in Academia.* Totowa, NJ: Rowman and Littlefield.

Campbell, D. J. (1969). Ethnocentrism of Disciplines and the Fish-Scale Model of Omniscience. In M. S. Sherif & C. W. Sherif (Eds.), *Interdisciplinary Relations in the Social Sciences* (pp. 328–348). Chicago: Aldine.

Carbone, P. F. (1980). Liberal Education and Teacher Preparation. *Journal of Teacher Education, 31*(3), 13–17.

Carnegie Commission on Higher Education. (1971). *From Isolation to Mainstream: Problems of the Colleges Founded for Negroes.* New York: McGraw-Hill.

Carnegie Commission on Higher Education. (1973). *Higher Education: Who Pays? Who Benefits?* New York: McGraw-Hill.

Carnegie Council on Policy Studies in Higher Education. (1976). *A Classification of Institutions of Higher Education.* Berkeley, CA: Author.

Carnegie Council on Policy Studies in Higher Education. (1980). *Three Thousand Futures: The Next Twenty Years for Higher Education.* San Francisco, CA: Jossey-Bass.

Carnegie Foundation for the Advancement of Teaching. (1977). *The Missions

of the College Curriculum: A Contemporary Review with Suggestions.
San Francisco: Jossey-Bass.

Carnegie Foundation for the Advancement of Teaching. (1987a). *A Classification of Institutions of Higher Education, 1987 Edition.* Princeton, NJ: Author.

Carnegie Foundation for the Advancement of Teaching. (1987b). Minority Access: A Question of Equity. *Change, 19*(3), 35–39.

Cassirer, E. (1950). *The Problem of Knowledge.* New Haven, CT: Yale University Press.

Cheney, L. V. (1989). *50 Hours: A Core Curriculum for College Students.* Washington, DC: National Endowment for the Humanities.

Churchill, J. (1983). Realism, Relativism, and the Liberal Arts. *Liberal Education, 67*(1), 33–44.

Clark, B. R. (1984). The Organizational Perspective. In B. R. Clark (Ed.), *Perspectives on Higher Education: Eight Disciplinary and Comparative Views* (pp. 106–131). Berkeley: University of California Press.

Clark, B. R. (1987). *The Academic Life: Small Worlds, Different Worlds.* Princeton, NJ: Carnegie Foundation for the Advancement of Teaching.

Commission for Educational Quality. (1985). *Improving Teacher Education: An Agenda for Higher Education and the Schools.* Atlanta, GA: Southern Regional Education Board.

Conrad, C. F., & Wyer, J. C. (1980). *Liberal Education in Transition* (AAHE-ERIC Higher Education Research Report No. 3). Washington, DC: American Association for Higher Education.

Cook, S. D. (1978). Politics and the Future of Black Colleges. *Journal of Black Studies, 2*(3), 173–181.

Council of State Governments. (1952). *Occupational Licensing Legislation in the United States.* Chicago: Author.

Cremin, L. A. (1961). *The Transformation of the School: Progressivism in American Education.* New York: Vintage Books.

Cross, K. P. (1986). A Proposal to Improve Teaching. *AAHE Bulletin, 39*(1), 9–14.

Crozier, M., Huntington, S., & Watanuki, J. (1975). *The Crisis of Democracy: Report on the Governability of Democracies to the Trilateral Commission.* New York: New York University Press.

Cullen, M. J. (1975). *The Statistical Movement in Early Victorian Britain: The Foundations of Empirical Social Research.* New York: Barnes & Noble.

Davidson, D. V., Dodson, H., & Ross, S. (Eds.). (1982). *Directory of Model Course Outlines in Black Studies. Vol. I: History and Political Economy; Vol. II: Cultural and Social Analysis.* Atlanta, GA: Institute of the Black World.

Davis, A. L. (1979). White Teachers at Black Colleges: A Case Study of Morehouse College. *Western Journal of Black Studies, 3*(3), 224–227.

Davis, K., & Moore, W. (1945). Some Principles of Stratification. *American Sociological Review, 10*(2), 242–249.

Davis, M. W. (1981). Concerns of Black Colleges about State Planning in Post-Secondary Education. *Journal of Negro Education, 50*(3), 237–250.

DeParle, J., & Mundy, L. (1989, October). Why Higher Education is Neither. *Washington Monthly*, pp. 33–39.

deYoung, A. (1989). *Economics and American Education*. New York: Longman.

Drake, St. C. (1955). The Social and Economic Status of the Negro in the United States. *Daedalus, 84*(4), 771–777.

Drake, St. C. (1971). The Black University in the American Social Order. *Daedalus, 100*(3), 833–897.

Dressel, P. L., & Marcus, D. (1982). *On Teaching and Learning in College*. San Francisco: Jossey-Bass.

Dressel, P. L., & Reichard, D. J. (1970). The University Department: Retrospect and Prospect. *Journal of Higher Education, 41*, 387–402.

Ducharme, E. (1980). Liberal Arts in Education: The Perennial Challenge. *Journal of Teacher Education, 31*(3), 7–12.

Dunham, E. A. (1969). *Colleges of the Forgotten Americans: A Profile of State Colleges and Regional Universities*. New York: McGraw-Hill.

Elam, D. M. (1978). Two Sides of the Coin: White Students in Black Institutions. *Journal of the National Association of Women Deans and Counselors, 41*(2), 66–71.

Elton, C. F. (1974). Black and White Colleges: A Comparative Perspective. *Journal of Negro Education, 43*(1), 111–116.

Euben, J. P. (1990). *The Tragedy of Political Theory: The Road Not Taken*. Princeton, NJ: Princeton University Press.

Fact File (Part 1). (1981a, June 15). *Chronicle of Higher Education*, p. 5.

Fact File (Part 2). (1981b, June 22). *Chronicle of Higher Education*, pp. 5–8.

Fethe, C. B. (1973). A Philosophical Model for Interdisciplinary Programs. *Liberal Education, 59*(4), 490–497.

Finkelstein, M. J. (1984). *The American Academic Profession: A Synthesis of Social Scientific Inquiry since World War II*. Columbus, Ohio: Ohio State University Press.

Fleming, J. (1984). *Blacks in College*. San Francisco: Jossey-Bass.

Flexner, A. (1915). *Is Social Work a Profession?* (Studies in Social Work No. 4). New York: New York School of Philanthropy.

Fussell, P. (1982, October 4). Schools for Snobbery. *The New Republic*, pp. 25–32.

Gaff, J. G. (1975). *Toward Faculty Renewal*. San Francisco: Jossey-Bass.

Gaff, J. G. (1983). *General Education Today: A Critical Analysis of Controversies, Practices, and Reforms*. San Francisco: Jossey-Bass.

Gaff, J. G. (1989). General Education at Decade's End: The Need for a Second Wave of Reform. *Change, 21*(4), 10–23.

Gamson, Z., and Associates. (1984). *Liberating Education*. San Francisco: Jossey-Bass.

Garver, E. (1986). Critical Thinking, Them, and Us: A Response to Arnold B.

Aaron's "Critical Thinking and the Baccalaureate Curriculum." *Liberal Education, 72*(3), 245-249.

Geiger, R. L. (1986). *To Advance Knowledge: The Growth of American Research Universities, 1900-1940.* New York: Oxford University Press.

Glazer, P. M., & Slater, M. (1987). *Unequal colleagues: The entrance of women into the professions.* New Brunswick, NJ: Rutgers University Press.

Godwin, W. L. (1971). Southern State Governments and Higher Education for Negroes. *Daedalus, 100*(3), 783-797.

Halstead, D. K. (1975). *Higher Education Prices and Price Indexes.* Washington, DC: U.S. Government Printing Office.

Halstead, D. K. (1980, October). Higher Education Prices and Price Indexes: 1980 Update. *Business Officer,* n.p.

Handlin, O., & Handlin, M. (1970). *The American College and American Culture: Socialization As a Function of Higher Education.* New York: McGraw-Hill.

Hansen, W. L. (1980). Regressing into the Eighties: Annual Report of the Economic Status of the Profession. *Academe: Bulletin of the AAUP, 66,* 267-278.

Hansen, W. L. (1986). Changes in Faculty Salaries. In H. Bowen & J. H. Schuster, *American Professors: A National Resource Imperiled* (pp. 80-112). New York: Oxford University Press.

Hansen, W. L., & Weisbrod, B. A. (1969). The Distribution of Costs and Direct Benefits of Public Higher Education: The Case of California. *Journal of Human Resources, 4*(2), 176-191.

Haskell, T. L. (1977). *The Emergence of Professional Social Science: The American Social Science Association and the Nineteenth-Century Crisis of Authority.* Urbana: University of Illinois Press.

Hausman, C. R. (1979). Introduction: Interdisciplinarity or Disciplinarity? In J. J. Kockelmans (Ed.), *Interdisciplinarity and Higher Education* (pp. 1-10). University Park: Pennsylvania State University Press.

Hawkins, H. (1979). University Identity: The Teaching and Research Functions. In A. Oleson & J. Voss (Eds.), *The Organization of Knowledge in Modern America, 1860-1920* (pp. 265-313). Baltimore: Johns Hopkins University Press.

Hawkins, H. (1983). A History of Creative Tensions. *Change, 15*(7), 34-37.

Hekman, S. (1983). *Weber's Ideal Type and Contemporary Social Theory.* Notre Dame, IN: Notre Dame Press.

Henry, D. D. (1975). *Challenges Past, Challenges Present: Analysis of American Higher Education Since 1930.* San Francisco: Jossey-Bass.

Herson, L. J. R. (1980). Helmsman, Bridge, and Cycle: The Liberal Arts Considered. *Journal of Teacher Education, 31*(3), 23-26.

Higham, J. (1979). The Matrix of Specialization. In A. Oleson & J. Voss (Eds.), *The Organization of Knowledge in Modern America, 1860-1920* (pp. 1-18). Baltimore: Johns Hopkins University Press.

Hill, P. (1981). Medium and Message in General Education. *Liberal Education*, *67*(2), 129-145.

Hill, S. T. (1981, September). Update on Black College Students and Black Colleges: 1980-81 [Entire issue]. *Bulletin of the National Center for Education Statistics* (NCES 81-361).

Hill, S. T. (1983, November). *Participation of Black Students in Higher Education: A Statistical Profile from 1970-71 to 1980-81* (Special Report, NCES 83-327). Washington, DC: U.S. Department of Education, National Center for Education Statistics.

Hirsch, E. D. (1987). *Cultural Literacy: What Every American Needs to Know*. Boston: Houghton-Mifflin.

Hodgkinson, H. L. (1983). *Guess Who's Coming to College? Your Students in 1990*. Washington, DC: National Association for Independent Colleges and Universities. (ERIC ED 225 497)

Hofstadter, R. (1962). *Anti-Intellectualism in American Life*. New York: Vintage Books.

Holmes Group. (1986). *Tomorrow's Teachers: A Report of the Holmes Group*. East Lansing, MI: Holmes Group.

Hook, S. (1946). *Education for Modern Man*. New York: Dial Press.

Huff, D. (1954). *How to Lie with Statistics*. New York: W. W. Norton.

Hutchins, R. M. (1936). *The Higher Learning in America*. New Haven, CT: Yale University Press.

Hutchins, R. (1968). *The Learning Society*. New York: Praeger.

Ivie, S. D. (1982). Why Black Students Score Poorly on the NTE. *High School Journal*, *65*(5), 169-175.

Jabs, A. E. (1973). On Being a White Professor in a Black College. *Negro Educational Review*, *24*(3-4), 138-143.

Jacoby, R. (1987). *The Last Intellectuals: American Culture in the Age of Academe*. New York: Basic Books.

Jencks, C., & Riesman, D. (1968). *The Academic Revolution*. New York: Doubleday.

Johnson, T. M. (1972). *Professions and Power*. London: Macmillan.

Jones, A. (1973). *Uncle Tom's Campus*. New York: Praeger.

Kates, G. (1989, July 5). The Classics of Western Civilization Do Not Belong to Conservatives Alone. *Chronicle of Higher Education*, p. B1.

Katz, J., & Henry, M. (1988). *Turning Professors into Teachers: A New Approach to Faculty Development and Student Learning*. New York: Macmillan.

Kavaloski, V. C. (1979). Interdisciplinary Education and Humanistic Aspiration. In J. J. Kockelmans (Ed.), *Interdisciplinarity and Higher Education* (pp. 224-243). University Park: Pennsylvania State University Press.

Keller, G. (1985). Trees Without Fruit: The Problem with Research about Higher Education. *Change*, *17*(1), 7-10.

Kerr, C. (1972). *The Uses of the University, with a Postscript—1972*. Cambridge, MA: Harvard University Press.

Kessell, R. A. (1958). Price Discrimination in Medicine. *Journal of Law and Economics, 1*(1), 20–53.

Kevles, D. (1979). The Physics, Mathematics, and Chemistry Communities: A Comparative Analysis. In A. Oleson & J. Voss (Eds.), *The Organization of Knowledge in Modern America, 1860–1920* (pp. 139–172). Baltimore: Johns Hopkins University Press.

Kimball, R. (1990). *Tenured Radicals: How Politics Corrupted Our Higher Education.* New York: Harper & Row.

Kingston, P. W. (1984). The Maintenance of Educational Hierarchy: Recent Trends in Where Blacks Go to College. *College and University, 60*(1), 37–53.

Klitgaard, R. G. (1985). *Choosing Elites.* Cambridge, MA: Ballinger Press.

Kolesnik, W. B. (1958). *Mental Discipline in Modern Education.* Madison: University of Wisconsin Press.

Krukowsi, J. (1985). What do Students Want? Status. *Choice, 17*(3), 21–28.

Kuh, G. D. (1981). *Indices of Quality in the Undergraduate Experience* (AAHE-ERIC Higher Education Report No. 4). Washington, DC: American Association of Higher Education.

Kuhn, T. (1962). *The Structure of Scientific Revolutions.* Chicago: University of Chicago Press.

Kurfiss, J. G. (1988). *Critical Thinking: Theory, Research, Practice, and Possibilities* (ASHE-ERIC Higher Education Report No. 2). Washington, DC: Association for the Study of Higher Education.

Ladd, E. C., & Lipset, S. M. (1975). *The Divided Academy: Professors and Politics.* New York: McGraw-Hill.

Lakatos, I. (1970). Falsification and the Methodology of Scientific Research Programmes. In A. Musgrave & I. Lakatos (Eds.), *Criticism and the Growth of Knowledge* (Proceedings of the International Colloquium in the Philosophy of Science, London, 1965; Vol. 4, pp. 91–196). Cambridge, England: Cambridge University Press.

Larson, M. S. (1977). *The Rise of Professionalism: A Sociological Analysis.* Berkeley: University of California Press.

Lasch, C. (1968). *The Culture of Narcissism.* New York: W. W. Norton.

Lawrence, J. K., & Green, K. C. (1980). *A Question of Quality: The Higher Education Ratings Game* (AAHE-ERIC Report 5). Washington, DC: American Association of Higher Education.

Lee, C. B. T. (1967). Knowledge Structure and Curriculum Development. In C. B. T. Lee (Ed.), *Improving College Teaching* (pp. 389–402). Washington, DC: American Council on Education.

Levine, D. O. (1986). *The American College and the Culture of Aspiration.* Ithaca, NY: Cornell University Press.

Levy, D. C. (1986). *Higher Education and the State in Latin America: Private Challenges to Public Dominance.* Chicago: University of Chicago Press.

Libarkin, B. (1984). A Study of the Satisfaction Levels of White Students at a Traditionally Black College. *Integrated Education, 22*(1–3), 89–94.

Light, D. W., Jr. (1974). The Structure of the Academic Professions. *Sociology of Education, 47*(1), 2–28.

Lincoln, C. E. (1971). The Negro Colleges and Cultural Change. *Daedalus, 100*(3), 603–629.

Lyson, T. A. (1983). The Changing Curriculum Orientations of Students at Black Land Grant Colleges: A Shift-Share Approach. *Research in Higher Education, 18*(4), 485–494.

Mannheim, K. (1936). *Ideology and Utopia*. New York: Harcourt, Brace, and World.

Martin, W. B. (1982). *The College of Character: Renewing the Purpose and Content of College Education*. San Francisco: Jossey-Bass.

Martins, P. F., & Brandt, N. (1976). *Financial Statistics of Institutions of Higher Education: Current Funds Revenues and Expenditures, 1972–1973*. Washington, DC: U.S. Government Printing Office.

Marx, K. (1843). On the Jewish Question. In T. B. Bottomore (Ed.), *Karl Marx: The Early Writings* (pp. 1–40). New York: McGraw-Hill.

Mauksch, H. (1980). What Are the Obstacles to Improving College Teaching? *Current Issues in Higher Education, 2*(1), 49–56.

McCauley, R. N. (1982). The Business of the University. *Liberal Education, 68*(1), 27–34.

McHenry, D. E. (Ed.). (1977). *Academic Departments: Problems, Variations, and Alternatives*. San Francisco: Jossey-Bass.

McPeck, J. E. (1981). *Critical Thinking and Education*. New York: St. Martin's Press.

McPherson, J. M. (1974). The New Puritanism: Values and Goals of Freedmen's Education in America. In L. Stone (Ed.), *The University in Society, Vol. II: Europe, Scotland, and the United States from the 16th to the 20th Century* (pp. 611–639). Princeton, NJ: Princeton University Press.

Meléndez, W. A., & de Guzmán, R. M. (1983). *Burnout: the New Academic Disease* (ASHE-ERIC Higher Education Report No. 9). Washington, DC: Association for the Study of Higher Education.

Metzger, W. P. (1965). The Age of the University. In R. Hofstadter & W. P. Metzger, *The Development of Academic Freedom in the United States* (pp. 407–605). New York: Columbia University Press.

Metzger, W. P. (Ed.). (1977). *Reader on the Sociology of the Academic Profession*. New York: Arno Press.

Metzger, W. P. (1987). The Academic Profession in the United States. In B. P. Clark (Ed.), *The Academic Profession: National, Disciplinary, and Institutional Settings* (pp. 123–208). Berkeley: University of California.

Miller, C. L. (1981). Higher Education for Black Americans: Problems and Issues. *Journal of Negro Education, 50*(3), 208–223.

Mitroff, I. I. (1982). Secure versus Insecure Forms of Knowing in University Settings: Two Archetypes of Inquiry. *Journal of Higher Education, 53*(6), 640–655.

Molnar, J. J., Dunkenberger, J. E., & Salter, D. A. (1980). Agricultural Education in the South: A Comparison of Student Characteristics at Land Grant Institutions. *Journal of Negro Education, 50*(1), 26–40.

Mommsen, K. G. (1973). Professionalism and the Racial Context of Career Patterns among Black American Doctorates: A Note on the "Brain Drain" Hypothesis. *Journal of Negro Education, 42*(2), 191–204.

Morrill, R. L. (1980). *Teaching Values in College.* San Francisco: Jossey-Bass.

Morris, A. (1981). *Equal Opportunity Scoreboard: The Status of Black Americans in Higher Education, 1970–79.* Washington, DC: Institute for the Study of Educational Policy at Howard University.

Morris, E. (1972). The Contemporary Negro College and the Brain Drain. *Journal of Negro Education, 41*(4), 309–319.

Morrison, J. (1973). *The Rise of the Arts on the American Campus.* New York: McGraw-Hill.

National Center for Education Statistics. (1980a). *Condition of Education, 1980.* Washington, DC: U.S. Government Printing Office.

National Center for Education Statistics. (1980b). *Digest of Education Statistics, 1980.* Washington, DC: U.S. Government Printing Office.

National Center for Education Statistics. (1985). *Historical Report: The Traditionally Black Institutions of Higher Education: Their Development and Status, 1860–1982.* Washington, DC: U.S. Department of Education.

Navin, L., & Magura, M. (1977). A Price Index for Universities' Budgetary Decisions. *Journal of Higher Education, 48*(2), 216–215.

Nelli, E. R. (1984). A Research Based Response to Allegations that Education Students Are Academically Inferior. *Action in Teacher Education, 6*(3), 73–80.

Newell, W. H. (1983). The Role of Interdisciplinary Studies in the Liberal Education of the 1980s. *Liberal Education, 69*(3), 245–256.

1986 Minority Enrollment at 3,200 Institutions of Higher Education. (1988, July 6). *Chronicle of Higher Education*, pp. A20–A29.

Ningard, E. (1982). The Experiences of Historically Black Colleges in Serving Diversely Prepared Students. *New Directions in Experiential Education, 17*, 29–36.

O'Keefe, M. (1985). What Ever Happened to the Crash of '80 '81 '82 '83 '84 '85? *Choice, 17*(3), 37–41.

O'Keefe, M. (1987). Where Does the Money Really Go? Case Studies of Six Institutions. *Change, 19*(6), 12–34.

O'Keefe, M. (1989). Private Colleges Beating the Odds/Despite Warnings, Enrollments Are Up. *Change, 21*(2), 9–19.

Oleson, A. M., & Voss, J. (Eds.). (1979). *The Organization of Knowledge in Modern America.* Baltimore: Johns Hopkins University Press.

Patterson, F. K., & Longsworth, C. R. (1966). *The Making of a College: Plans for a New Departure in Higher Education.* Cambridge, MA: MIT Press.

Peeps, J. M. S. (1981). Northern Philanthropy and the Emergence of Black Higher Education—Do-Gooders, Compromisers, or Co-Conspirators? *Journal of Negro Education, 50*(3), 251–269.

Perkins, H. (1984). The Historical Perspective. In B. R. Clark (Ed.), *Perspectives on Higher Education: Eight Disciplinary and Comparative Views* (pp. 33–39). Berkeley, CA: University of California Press.

Perry, W. G. (1981). Cognitive and Ethical Growth: The Making of Meaning. In A. W. Chickering (Ed.), *The Modern American College* (pp. 76–116). San Francisco: Jossey-Bass.

Phenix, P. (1962). The Use of the Disciplines As Curriculum Content. *Educational Forum, 26*(3), 273–280.

Pickle, J. (1984). Relationships Between Knowledge and Learning Environments in Teacher Education. *Journal of Teacher Education, 35*(5), 13–17.

Pietig, J. (1984). Is Education a Discipline? *Educational Forum, 48*(3), 365–372.

Powell, C. N. (1981). A Study to Determine the Influence of Certain Non-Cognitive Factors on Achievement of Freshmen Students Enrolled in a Predominantly Black State Supported College. *Negro Educational Review, 32*(2), 38–45.

Preer, J. L. (1982). *Lawyers v. Educators: Black Colleges and Desegregation in Public Higher Education.* Westport, CT: Greenwood Press.

President's Commission on Foreign Languages and International Studies. (1979). *Strength Through Wisdom: A Critique of U.S. Capability.* Washington, DC: Author.

Project on Redefining the Meaning and Purpose of Baccalaureate Degrees. (1985). *Integrity in the College Curriculum: A Report to the Academic Community.* Washington, DC: American Association of Colleges.

Ravitch, D., & Finn, C., Jr. (1987). *What Our Seventeen Year Olds Know: A Report on the First National Assessement of History and Literature.* New York: Harper & Row.

Rehnke, M. A. F. (1982–1983). Liberal Learning and Career Preparation: An Introduction. *Current Issues in Higher Education, 2*(1–3), 1–9.

Rich, J. M. (1980). A Rationale for the Liberal Education of Educators. *Journal of Teacher Education, 31*(3), 27–30.

Rice, R. E. (1983). *Strategies for Relating Career Preparation and Liberal Learning.* St. Paul, MN: Northwest Area Foundation Report.

Riesman, D. (1956). *Constraint and Variety in American Education.* Lincoln: University of Nebraska Press.

Riesman, D. (1980). *On Higher Education: the Academic Enterprise in an Era of Rising Student Consumerism.* San Francisco: Jossey-Bass.

Rosenblatt, S. (1989). Merits and Defects: the American Education System. *Liberal Education, 75*(1), 18–23, 49.

Ross, D. (1979). The Development of the Social Sciences. In A. Oleson & J. Voss (Eds.), *The Organization of Knowledge in Modern America, 1860–1920* (pp. 107–138). Baltimore: The Johns Hopkins University Press.

Rossides, D. W. (1984). What Is the Purpose of Education? The Worthless Debate Continues. *Change, 16*(3), 14–21, 44–46.

Rudolph, F. (1962). *The American College and University.* New York: Knopf.

Rudolph, F. (1977). *Curriculum: A History of the American Undergraduate Course of Study Since 1636.* San Francisco: Jossey-Bass.

Ruscio, K. P. (1987). Many Sectors, Many Professions. In B. P. Clark (Ed.), *The Academic Profession: National, Disciplinary, and Institutional Settings* (pp. 371–400). Berkeley, CA: University of California Press.

Selin, H. (1988). Teaching Research Methods to Undergraduates. *College Teaching, 36*(20), 54–56.

Shannon, S. S. (1982). Land-Grant College Legislation and Black Tennesseans: A Case Study in the Politics of Education. *History of Education Quarterly, 22*(2), 139–157.

Shimeall, K. M. (1980). Merger as a Remedy in Higher Education Desegregation: Greier *v.* University of Tennessee. *University of Toledo Law Review, 11*(3), 511–538.

Shor, I. (1980). *Critical Teaching and Everyday Life.* Boston: South End Press.

Shulman, C. H. (1979). *Old Expectations, New Realities: The Academic Profession Revisited* (AAHE-ERIC Higher Education Research Report No. 2). Washington, DC: American Association for Higher Education.

Smith, J. Z. (1983). Why the College Major? Questioning the Great Unexplained Aspect of Undergraduate Education. *Change, 15*(5), 12–15.

Sorkin, A. (1969). A Comparison of Quality Characteristics in Negro and White Colleges and Universities in the South. *Journal of Negro Education, 38*(1), 112–119.

Stadtman, V. A. (1980). *Academic Adaptations: Higher Education Prepares for the 1980s and 1990s.* San Francisco: Jossey-Bass.

Standley, N. S. (1978). *White Students Enrolled in Black Colleges and Universities.* Atlanta: Southern Regional Educational Board.

Stent, M. D. (1984). Black College Involvement in International and Cross-Cultural Education. In A. Garibaldi (Ed.), *Black Colleges and Universities; Challenges for the Future* (pp. 93–115). New York: Praeger.

Straus, R. (1973, November 30). Departments and Disciplines: Stasis and Change. *Science,* pp. 895–897.

Stringer, P. (1974). White Teachers, Black Campus. *Change, 6*(9), 27–31.

Study Group on the Conditions of Excellence in American Higher Education. (1984). *Involvment in Learning: Realizing the Potential of American Higher Education.* Washington, DC: U.S. Department of Education, National Institute of Education.

Swora, T., & Morrison, J. (1974). Interdisciplinarity and Higher Education. *Liberal Education, 60*(1), 45–52.

Thompson, D. C. (1984). Research Areas for Black Colleges. In A. Garibaldi (Ed.), *Black Colleges and Universities: Challenges for the Future* (pp. 137–152). New York: Praeger.

Thorpe, M. D. (1975). The Future of Black Colleges and Universities in the Desegregation and Integration Process. *Journal of Black Studies, 6*(1), 100–112.

Thurow, L. (1975). *Generating Inequality: Mechanisms of Distribution in the U.S. Economy.* New York: Basic Books.

Tierney, W. G. (1989). *Curricular Landscapes, Democratic Vistas: Transformative Leadership in Higher Education.* New York: Praeger.

Tollett, K. S. (1982). *Black Colleges as Instruments of Affirmative Action* (Occasional Paper No. 4). Washington, DC: Institute for the Study of Educational Policy.

Toulmin, S., & Goodfield, G. J. (1962). *The Architecture of Matter.* New York: Harper and Row.

Trow, M. (1984). The Analysis of Status. In B. R. Clark (Ed.), *Perspectives on Higher Education: Eight Disciplinary and Comparative Views* (pp. 132–143). Berkeley: University of California Press.

Trow, M. (1984-1985). Interdisciplinary Study As a Counterculture: Problems of Birth, Growth, and Survival. *Issues in Integrative Studies* (3), 1–16.

Uhl, N. P. (1978). A Case Study of Goals-Oriented Research. *New Directions for Institutional Research, 3*(5), 61–77.

U.S. Bureau of the Census. (1975). *Historical Statistics of the United States, Colonial Times to 1970* (Bicentennial Edition, Part 1). Washington, DC: U.S. Government Printing Office.

U.S. National Commission on Excellence in Education. (1983). *A Nation at Risk: The Imperative for Educational Reform.* Washington, DC: Author.

U.S. Suggests Settlement of Ala. Desegregation Case. (1985, July 3). *Chronicle of Higher Education,* p. 2.

Veysey, L. R. (1965). *The Emergence of the American University.* Chicago: University of Chicago Press.

Veysey, L. R. (1973). Stability and Experiment in the American Undergraduate Curriculum. In C. Kaysen (Ed.), *Content and Context: Essays on College Education* (pp. 1–64). New York: McGraw-Hill for the Carnegie Commission on Higher Education.

Veysey, L. R. (1978). *The Humanities in American Universities Since the 1930s: The Decline of Grandiosity.* Unpublished manuscript, University of California, Santa Cruz.

Veysey, L. R. (1979). The Plural Organized World of the Humanities. In A. Oleson & J. Voss (Eds.), *The Organization of Knowledge in Modern America, 1860-1920* (pp. 51–106). Baltimore: Johns Hopkins University Press.

Walters, K. S. (1986). Critical Thinking in Liberal Education: A Case of Overkill? *Liberal Education, 72*(3), 233–244.

Warnat, W. I. (1976). The Role of White Faculty on the Black Campus. *Journal of Negro Education, 45*(3), 334–338.

Wasserman, P., & Bernero, J. (1977). *Statistics Sources* (5th ed.). Detroit: Gale.

Watkins, B. T. (1985, June 19). Faculty Members at Liberal-Arts Colleges Searching for a New Definition of Success: Many Are Torn Between Old Loyalty to Academic Discipline and New Orientation to Teaching. *Chronicle of Higher Education,* pp. 23, 25.

Weathersby, G. R. (1984, January–February). Our Fading State Colleges: Have They Lost Their Vitality and Mission? *Change, 16*, 18–13, 49.

Weaver, F. S. (1980). *Class, State, and Industrial Structure: The Historical Process of Industrial Growth in South America.* Westport, CT: Greenwood.

Weaver, F. S. (1981). Academic Disciplines and Undergraduate Liberal Arts Education. *Liberal Education, 67*(2), 151–165.

Weaver, F. S. (1984). Disciplinary Professionalism: One View of the Developing Context for Alternative Colleges. In R. Jones & B. Smith (Eds.), *Against the Current: Reform and Experimentation in Higher Education* (pp. 3–17). Cambridge, MA: Schenkman.

Weaver, F. S. (Ed.). (1989). *Promoting Inquiry in Undergraduate Learning* (New Directions in Teaching and Learning, No. 38). San Francisco: Jossey-Bass.

Weaver, F. S., & Weaver, S. A. (1979). For Public Libraries the Poor Pay More. *Library Journal, 104*(3), 352–355.

Webb, R. B., & Sherman, R. R. (1983). Liberal Education: An Aim for Colleges of Education. *Journal of Teacher Education, 34*(4), 23–26.

Weber, S. L. (1983). Liberal Learning: A Learned Ignorance. *Liberal Education, 69*(1), 75–80.

Webster, D. S. (1981). Black Student Elite: Enrollment Shifts of Higher Achieving, High Socio-Economic Status Black Students from Black to White Colleges During the 1970s. *College and University, 56*(3), 283–291.

Webster, D. S. (1984). Chicano Students in American Higher Education. *Integrated Education, 22*(1–3), 41–52.

Wegener, C. (1978). *Liberal Education and the Modern University.* Chicago: University of Chicago Press.

Weinberg, M. (1977). *A Chance to Learn: A History of Race and Education in the United States.* Cambridge, England: Cambridge University Press.

White, E. M., & Ahrens, R. (1989). European vs. American Higher Education: Two Issues and a Clear Winner. *Change, 21*(5), 52–55.

Wilensky, H. L. (1970). The Professionalization of Everyone? *American Journal of Sociology, 70*(3), 137–158.

Williams, G. (1984). The Economic Approach. In B. R. Clark (Ed.), *Perspectives on Higher Education: Eight Disciplinary and Comparative Views* (pp. 79–105). Berkeley: University of California Press.

Williams, J. B. (1984). Public Policy and Black College Development: An Agenda for Research. In A. Garibaldi (Ed.), *Black Colleges and Universities: Challenges for the Future* (pp. 178–198). New York: Praeger.

Wisniewski, R. (1982). Three Scenarios for Teacher Education. *Journal of Teacher Education, 33*(2), 2–6.

Woditsch, G. A., Schlesinger, M. A., & Giardina, R. C. (1987). The Skillful Baccalaureate: Doing What Liberal Education Does Best. *Change, 19*(6), 48–57.

Wolff, R. P. (1987). Review of *The Closing of the American Mind* by Allan Bloom. *Academe, 73*(5), 64–65.

Yuker, H. E. (1984). *Faculty Workload: Research, Theory, and Interpretation* (ASHE-ERIC Higher Education Research Report No. 10). Washington, DC: Association for the Study of Higher Education.

Zeichner, K. M. (1983). Alternative Paradigms of Teacher Education. *Journal of Teacher Education, 34*(3), 3-9.

Zeisel, H. (1968). *Say It with Figures* (5th ed.). New York: Harper & Row.

Zingg, P. J. (1983). The Three Myths of Professionalization. *Liberal Education, 69*(3), 215-224.

Index

189

About the Author

Frederick Stirton Weaver is a professor of economics and history at Hampshire College, where he has served as Dean of the School of Social Science, Director of Institutional Research, and Coordinator of Third World Studies. He earned his B.A. in economics from the University of California at Berkeley and Ph.D. in economics from Cornell University. He is the editor of *Promoting Inquiry in Undergraduate Learning* (1989) and the author of *Regional Patterns of Economic Change in Chile, 1950-1964* (1968), *Class, State, and Industrial Structure* (1980), a historical study of Central American political economy (forthcoming), and numerous articles on Latin American economic history and development and U.S. higher education. Under the auspices of the Fulbright Commission, he recently worked as a consultant with four Ecuadorian universities.